All Things
Considered

All Things Considered

ROY BONISTEEL

Doubleday Canada Limited

Canadian Cataloguing in Publication Data

Bonisteel, Roy
   All things considered

Hardcover ISBN 0-385-25599-3; Paperback ISBN 0-385-25728-7

1. Spirituality. 2. Christian life. I. Title.

BV4510.2.B66 1997   248   C97-930549-7

Cover photograph by Johnnie Eisen
Front cover design by Tania Craan
Text design by Heidy Lawrance Associates
Printed and bound in the USA

Published in Canada by
Doubleday Canada Limited
105 Bond Street
Toronto, Ontario
M5B 1Y3

BVG 10 9 8 7 6 5 4 3 2 1

CONTENTS

ACKNOWLEDGEMENTS

Thanks to the family — Mandy, Steven and Therese, Lesley, Jane and all other kith and kin who participated actively or gave moral support to this endeavour. I'm a family kind of guy and I've got the best in the world. Appreciation is also expressed to Muriel Duncan and her staff at the *United Church Observer* for permission to reprint many of these columns and to John Pearce of Doubleday Canada, who is an author's best friend. In one of these columns I pay tribute to editors who have rescued me over the years. I would add Anne Holloway, Shaun Oakey and Christine Innes to that list. Thanks also to the readers of the *Observer* who wrote letters over the years in response to my columns and who suggested that they be compiled in a book.

This book is dedicated to
F.A.C.E. (Families and Children Experiencing) AIDS
In hope.

PREFACE

It seems I have always written columns of one kind or another. My first newspaper job in the early '50s was with my home town paper and involved, along with covering the town council meetings and Ladies' Aid bake sales, writing a series on local history. This wasn't too difficult since our family had lived in the area for seven generations and stories of pioneer derring-do came with mother's milk. What I couldn't pick up from family and neighbours I gleaned from our small lending library. I learned how to dig for little-known facts, search out confirmation and most of all, with the help of a remarkable editor, how to be concise.

When I began a radio career later in the '50s, I still wrote a weekly newspaper column about the programs and personalities from the world of broadcasting. These were the juicy tidbits that served as promotion for the radio station, which, incidentally, was owned by the newspaper. Over the many years I spent in television at the Canadian Broadcasting Corporation, my columns became more serious and took the form of commentaries and editorials. It was demanded of me that I have an opinion on just about everything, whether I did or not.

When I left the CBC I was asked by my son, at that time an editor at the *Kingston Whig-Standard*, to write a monthly column about my growing-up years in the Quinte area of Ontario. These were published in that paper in almanac fashion, describing life on the family farm. Doubleday Canada collected them in a book called *There Was a Time . . .* and published it in 1990. I have recently recorded the book on tape and it has been issued with original music by Andy Thompson.

My first column for the *United Church Observer*, published in March 1990, was called "Human Worth Is Much More Than Skin-Deep." It is also the first one in this book. The rest are presented here not in chronological order, but organized in chapters according to their subject matter. For that reason, to help put the material in context, the date the column first appeared is included. When the *Observer* approached me to do a regular column, I asked what it should be about. Editor Muriel Duncan said, "Write about anything you like. Try and make them not as soft as your reminiscences in *There Was a Time*, and not as tough as your CBC radio editorials."

I've tried to find the happy medium and so far she hasn't

complained, which is more than I can say for my readers. When I wrote the column "Mixing Alcohol with a Little Common Sense," I thought I was railing against hypocrisy, but the flood of letters took me to task for promoting drinking. After my column "Male by Birth, Feminist by Choice" I was criticized for trying to see the world through the eyes of women. Most, however, like the reader who said she was going to frame my column "The Joys of Making and Breaking Bread," have responded with warmth and affection. Some readers have complained that secular writers have no place in a church magazine. That the *United Church Observer* has always published articles of a more worldly nature, written by freelance writers and staff, along with its reverent and doctrinal material is what has made it one of Canada's most highly respected and relevant magazines.

I will probably always write columns because it is one of the best ways to keep in touch with people. Most readers, I am sure, like columns because they are short. Generally, they fit on one page of a newspaper or magazine, often with a smiling face at the top as a friendly reminder of stability in a rapidly changing world.

Like shooting arrows in the air, now and again a column will land in the right place. It will make an impression, cause a response, perhaps even change a mind. I have read some memorable columns over the years, written very few, but they remain my favourite writing genre — all things considered.

1

BEAUTIFUL PEOPLE

"Beware, as long as you live,
of judging people by appearances."

— JEAN DE LA FONTAINE (1621–95)

Human Worth Is Much More Than Skin-Deep
MARCH 1990

I have been wondering if there are a lot of people today who would like to look different than they do. This is on my mind because of something I received in the mail the other day.

It was a personally addressed letter from a well-known Canadian advertising agency on behalf of a professional counsellor offering me psychological help after plastic surgery. The letter pointed out that last year more than 10,000 women in this country had breast enlargement operations and that nose restructuring and facelifts have become very popular. More and more, men are also having cosmetic surgery.

My first reaction was, "Where did they get my name? Why are they writing to me?" Did they see me on television or in the newspaper and decide, "Wow, there's a face that could use some major repair"?

The letter said: "Cosmetic surgery was once reserved for Hollywood stars and the very wealthy, but today it is becoming increasingly accessible to many middle-class Canadians." Perhaps that's my answer. I'm simply on the mailing list of "middle-class Canadians" and the letter wasn't aimed specifically at me. Maybe they think rich people already have had it done and poor people don't want to look pretty.

I took a long look in the mirror. No doubt about it, the face looks like five miles of bad road, but then, it always has. If I had the wrinkles puffed up, the nose shortened, the ears pinned back and the warts removed it certainly would look better ... but it wouldn't be me.

I remember a television program I did many years ago with a woman named Sondra Diamond. She had suffered all her life from cerebral palsy, was unable to walk or move with any coordination. She talked with great difficulty and her body twitched uncontrollably. As a teenager, she was trapped in a fire and received burns to over 50 per cent of her body. When I met her she was 37 years old and had battled her way through life with incredible bravery and intelligence. She had a PhD in psychology, knew exactly who she was and had no illusions about how she looked.

We talked about humanness. She said, "To come to an understanding of humanness, the only essential thing is to make no assumptions. Don't decide by how a person looks. Our society says we must have a beautiful body, blue eyes, blond hair and be structurally straight. You are expected to do certain self-help tasks, toilet yourself, feed yourself, things I cannot do, and I certainly don't have a beautiful body. It means living up to other people's expectations. We have not developed sophisticated enough instruments yet to measure humanness. We don't know what's going on inside a person. I am not what you see."

The avalanche of letters received after the program went on the air made one fact very clear. Everyone who saw her agreed that Sondra was a very beautiful person. Even today, years later, people I meet remember what she said and how she helped them take a deeper look at themselves and the people around them.

I think most of us believe in the old maxims that "Beauty is in the eye of the beholder," or "Beauty is only skin-deep," but we still support an industry intent on carving us into pretty shapes.

I realize that cosmetic surgery is a tremendous benefit to many people, especially those born with some deformity or who have been accidentally disfigured. Certainly psychological help is a good idea before and after this type of operation. But do we really need therapists hiring ad agencies to drum up unsolicited business for themselves and the medical profession?

I'm delighted new medical technology is available for those in need. What I don't appreciate is seeing it commercially huckstered like a new brand of toothpaste.

Sometimes it seems as if stories about triumphant people like Sondra Diamond never make it into the mainstream media. Instead, our newspapers present an increasingly horrific stream of articles about violence and mayhem while a plethora of television talk shows thrive on a diet of the perverse and sadistic.

I definitely think it is time for some good news. So, let me tell you about Sandy Mitchell.

A Small Oasis of Good News
JUNE 1996

Sandy Mitchell was born in Scotland 50 years ago to a rather well-off family with a high social profile. His father had difficulty acknowledging the fact that his son had cerebral palsy. The boy's speech impediments and spasticity were an embarrassment. He was hidden away for a number of years in Down's syndrome communities and special schools in Scotland, Bermuda and the United States. It wasn't until his mid-thirties that he was able to overcome much of his life's early trauma and develop what he calls a sense of inner resourcefulness.

"Ultimately I changed from being someone who was frightened to go into a shop alone," Sandy told me, "into a person who wouldn't bat an eyelid at getting on a plane and finding my own way from the airport to where I wanted to go."

Luckily for us, one place he wanted to go was Canada.

Sandy's love of agriculture and a deep empathy for those with disabilities has resulted in Windreach, 105 acres in the rolling countryside north of Port Hope, Ontario. He has developed it into a completely accessible farm environment and nature interpretation centre, especially designed for disabled individuals and small groups. For Sandy it's a dream come true. "It has been my lifelong desire to be close to the land," he says.

Part of the desire was to provide a similar opportunity for others. Paths and ramps are designed for wheelchairs and walkers. The animals come to you to be petted. The fruit trees are of the dwarf variety for easy low-level picking. Flower, vegetable and herb garden plots are elevated to allow close enjoyment. A full-sized farm wagon is designed to accommodate a number of wheelchairs for a hay ride over the fields and through the woods.

People who seldom get a chance to leave their institution, school or nursing home discover what a baby lamb feels like or taste a just-picked cob of corn. "I have often seen some just sitting on a bench in the sun or in the shade of the gazebo with tears in their eyes, just enjoying the smells and sounds of the farm," reports Sandy.

An accessible playground was installed. An agricultural museum will be opened in the upper barn, a woodworking shop is being planned and a canteen will be available. The chicks and ducklings will be hatching this month. Three new calves are expected before July and two angora goats have been donated. Sandy is beaming.

Windreach was founded in 1984. The first year only a few people came, then as word got out, numbers increased. Last year 3,854 visitors enjoyed the calm, quiet ambience of country life on a working farm. Sandy has had to hire three full-time staff members and has welcomed many volunteers.

It's a commitment, he says, to preserve the circle of life and to welcome to that circle those who, because of disability, are frequently denied the opportunity.

There is no cost to visit Windreach. It's a gift from Sandy.

Beacons of Warmth and Welcome
JANUARY 1994

It never ceases to amaze me how a person's kind word or action can have such a lasting impact. I recall a letter from a reader of my columns who said, "This letter is long overdue, 20 years to be exact."

She went on to explain that on January 1, 1972, she and her husband were travelling on a major Canadian highway when their car, an old '62 Chevy, broke down. "Car after car whizzed by but no one stopped. It was beginning to get cold and darkness was falling when we finally decided to seek help at a farmhouse. I remember how frightened we were. Although we were in our early twenties, we were just kids and had no experience dealing with such emergencies.

"We knocked at the first farmhouse we came to, not knowing what reception to expect. When we were asked to come in we found two couples sitting down to their New Year's dinner. The hostess must have sensed our anxiety for she did everything possible to make us feel comfortable. We were allowed to use the telephone to call the police for a tow and then were asked to stay for dinner. We declined because we were concerned the tow would arrive while we were away, but we did enjoy a wonderful piece of cherry cheesecake. When we went back out into the cold we didn't feel quite so lonely or frightened.

Eventually a tow came, we continued to our destination by taxi and went on with our lives."

My correspondent goes on to tell what has happened to her in the intervening 20 years. Marriage break-up, remarriage "to a wonderful man," the birth of two children, a challenging career and the publication of seven books are described with pride and warmth. She tells of her drifting away from her United Church upbringing then finding her way back with the help of a United Church minister and his wife who became like second parents.

"I am sending this letter to you because I am certain you were a guest at the farmhouse we visited so long ago. I recognized you then as being on television but could not recall your name. I later learned that you lived in that area. If you think I am correct and know which family helped us would you please convey to them a long-overdue thank you. I'm sure from their point of view it was simply a matter of rural hospitality but the memory of that safe haven from the darkness of the highway has lasted with me all these years.

"Although you and the others at the table that January 1, 1972, will likely not even recall the incident, please convey my appreciation nonetheless."

My neighbours and lifelong friends, Arnold and Betty, lived for many years on the heritage family farm, which was sliced in two by a major highway route. The lights of the old homestead were welcoming beacons to many a stranded traveller over those years. Hardly a week went by when someone didn't come to the door to seek shelter or assistance. They have since moved to a new home on a different part of the same farm, further away from the highway, and are still a vital part of our small community. Twenty years ago when our children were about the same age we shared many a family time together, including New Year's 1972.

I took the letter over for them to read. We all remembered the dinner, but couldn't recall the night visitors.

"There were so many of them," said Arnold. "Some just wanted to use the phone, others had been in accidents and needed blankets or clothes. We just did what we could."

I pointed to the last paragraph of the letter. It read, "My only regret is that now, 20 years later, I wonder if your friends would make the same decision about strangers coming to the door. Modern realities have made Christian acts of kindness a matter of calculated risk rather than the natural thing to do."

Without hesitation Betty said, "Of course we would do the same. Times may change but people really don't. I still make a great cherry cheesecake and I'm more than happy to share a slice or two."

Every New Year's Day journalists publish a list of prominent people who died the preceding year. Some are entertainers or sports figures who have given us a great deal of pleasure, some are individuals who have affected us more deeply. In 1991, I recalled two people who had made a profound impression on me.

Two Who Made Life Richer for All of Us
JANUARY 1991

In 1990, the death of Bruno Bettelheim, the famous American analyst and Viennese-born child psychologist, recalled to me some time we had spent together two decades before.

Using fantasy and children's fairy tales as symbols, Bettelheim talked about hope and meaning in modern life. He said, "The greatest value of the fairy tale is that it gives hope. Cinderella feels persecuted by the stepmother and her evil sisters. But the difference is that, while Cinderella is persecuted, there is always hope and because of this she is rescued.

"Many fairy stories," he said, "such as Hansel and Gretel, Snow White and others, are about people lost in the forest. These are very ancient symbols of humankind in crisis; mental crisis, emotional crisis and moral crisis of being lost and not knowing which way to turn. These are the same developmental crisis we all go through as we move out of childhood into adolescence, out of adolescence into maturity. Before Snow White is kicked out by her stepmother she didn't work. She didn't do anything. She had a jolly good time. Then comes the crisis. She is lost in the forest. She is lost in an entirely different workaday world of the seven dwarfs. Then she meets the temptation of the queen and she falls for it.

"It is no different today. We all need help in coping with the problems of life. Look at all the successful books telling us how to cope. Look at the encounter groups, therapy sessions and spread of cults, which shows that people are looking beyond the immediate present and harsh reality in which we all live our lives. Many people feel a great drought because life has become meaningless to them. A fairy story offers hope. It tells us that a happy ending is available if you struggle hard enough, if you don't give up and if you try to do the right thing."

Many people will find these words ironic, since Bruno Bettelheim's death notice stated that at the age of 87 he took his own life. We will never know what terrors led to that decision, but I am profoundly sorry that there was no one there to offer him gentle wisdom and compassionate insight with which he saved countless lives.

That same year, broadcaster Malcolm Muggeridge, one of Britain's best known and most controversial journalists, died. I first met him in 1968 and over the years interviewed him on several occasions, spending time at his home near the small village of Robertsbridge. Our last conversation was about coping with life's vicissitudes.

He said, "I can't see any basis in which a person could regard life as sacred if it is seen as merely a part of an animal set-up. For me life is something that deserves our infinite respect and we are not in a position, under any circumstances, to judge its quality or necessity. Life is sacred because it is created by God for a purpose and that purpose comes to an end when you die. It is not for you to say 'I don't want to live,' because it is not your notion that is being worked out. It's part of the purpose of the Creator and that alone makes it your duty to live out your life. I see life in the setting of a divine creation which partakes of eternity as well as time." He too died at 87, three months after suffering a stroke.

Bettelheim and Muggeridge. Two highly individual men who died the same year at the same age. They lived and died in different ways but they were united in the conviction that life should be lived to the fullest.

We don't always have to look to the international scene for examples of how to live life. There have been many Canadians who knew how to seize the day.

Memories of Two Modern-Day Saints
JANUARY 1992

In 1991 Paul-Émile Cardinal Léger and Dr. Robert McClure died within days of each other after long lives of selfless dedication to others. Editorial writers have called them "modern-day saints." While this is probably true, I know how embarrassing both of them would find that appellation.

My memories of them will always be of their profound simplicity and their bubbling sense of humour. They were fun people to be around; they were good company. These two, who likely saw more of the world's suffering and hardship than most people would see in ten lifetimes, managed to exude a sense of optimism and good cheer whenever we met.

I first met Cardinal Léger in the fall of 1969. He had returned to Canada after two years in Africa to launch a fundraising tour for his leprosy clinics. The press was full of reports describing his near exhaustion and frail condition. I was scheduled to interview him at the Queen Elizabeth Hotel in Montreal. On our way to the meeting, CBC-Television producer Louise Lore and I discussed the correct protocol to observe when meeting a cardinal.

"Does one curtsy to a cardinal or kiss his ring?" wondered Louise.

"I don't know," I replied. " I once met Cardinal Flahiff of Winnipeg, but that was at a party and I didn't know he was a cardinal until someone told me. "

We needn't have worried. As we came through the door of the hotel with our TV equipment, the cardinal spotted us from across the lobby. He strode up to Louise, threw his arms around her in a warm bear-hug, thrust a hand out to me and beamed, "Welcome to Montreal. I'm Léger."

He loved to tell stories about the people of his Christian community in Cameroon where he was called Koo Koo Ma, which means man who has power. The exercise of his power meant more to his people than it did to him, but he loved their spirit.

"When I visit a village for a service they insist on singing every hymn they know for me. This can take hours. When I walk from the church to the house where I am staying they all want to touch me. They don't kiss my ring as people do in Canada. They bite my fingers. There is much joy and happiness and straightforward love."

Bob McClure was also a great storyteller. He used his tales as modern parables to make a point or to reveal a truth. I travelled quite a bit with Bob to meetings or speaking engagements and never tired of hearing even his tallest tales over and over. And that's not to say he couldn't be original. Once at a meeting where a certain amount of wrangling was going on over minor details of church union, I heard him remark, "In India we had Protestant missionaries working with Hindu Indians drilling wells for thirsty people with a drill rig that was purchased by Catholics. And you know, the water that came up was completely non-denominational."

In Calgary one time, we were both speaking at the same convention. The microphone in the auditorium had been giving me problems during the day and I had complained loudly and publicly several times. In the evening I was asked to introduce "the moderator of the United Church of Canada," which I did with proper solemnity. Down the aisle he came to the gasps of the crowd. Instead of the traditional black gown, he was wearing denim coveralls and a hard construction hat and carrying a screwdriver, a monkey wrench and a hammer. He marched up to the microphone, which was now working beautifully, gave it a couple of short taps and said, "You see, Roy, if something goes wrong with the system, fix it. It's a waste of time to complain. The problems of this world will never be solved by expecting someone else to fix things. We have to do it ourselves."

With this visual demonstration, his good-humoured chastisement of me, and the crowd in the palm of his hand, he then doffed his hardhat and proceeded with his usual stirring address.

McClure and Léger, saints? It depends on your definition. And perhaps the best definition I've heard was from a little girl whose only exposure to saints was seeing them portrayed in the stained-glass windows of her church. When asked by her priest, "What is a saint?" she answered, "They are people the light shines through."

That certainly applies in these cases.

A Divine Spark in Danger of Fading Away

APRIL 1995

The *United Church Observer* once featured a beautiful multicoloured front cover that folded out to reveal a promotional piece for the Mission and Service Fund. On the inside fold were these words: "Deep inside us there's a divine spark, or perhaps it's a raging fire, that says, I want to make a difference with my life. I don't want to just take, I want to give. I don't want to tear down and use up, I want to build and heal."

There was no attribution for these words but they could easily have been written by my friend George. George has been saying that to me for many months. The problem is, he can't find anyone to take what he wants to give.

He has worked hard all his life, lived frugally, invested wisely and now, at the age of 83, finds himself with an estate of over $2.5 million. A widower with no children, he and his late wife had a dream. They pictured a camp for underprivileged children on a 203-acre farm they owned. It would be an ideal setting with rolling hills, sparkling streams and towering trees in a beautiful part of Canada. When his wife died George tried harder than ever to bring that dream to reality as a memorial to her and to satisfy a burning desire to give back to his community some of the blessings they had both enjoyed. But he discovered how difficult it is to give.

He approached the provincial government with his offer to build a camp, donating the property, but found a complete lack of interest. He investigated the possibilities with some Pentecostal organizations to no effect. He tried the United Church but was told it was having a tough time keeping its existing camps afloat. The Salvation Army seemed encouraging but continually delayed any decision.

All of the churches were quite happy to take possession of his property and his money but wanted the right to use it as they saw fit. Some merely suggested he bequeath his estate to them in his will. George, perhaps correctly, envisioned his wealth ending up in some denomination's head office instead of being used in the community.

About a year ago, he contacted me to see if I could help him with his dilemma.

We had never met before and I made the trip to his modest but comfortable home curious about what sort of man I would find. As he poured out his story, I found a sincere, caring, but lonely man, very aware of the approaching end of life and eager to leave something tangible before he went. "All I have asked is for people to come with their hand out and I would fill it," he laments. True to his words, he makes very generous donations to many churches and charitable organizations each year. Tax collectors, lawyers and accountants of course get their share.

I have not been much help. I managed to put him in touch with people who have offered to create a foundation from which he can distribute funds for the use of deserving children.

This may be the best way to go. The only other thing I do is provide a listening ear — he loves to "visit" — and keep an eye on his failing health. While distance is a problem, we manage to get together about once a month. I always come away inspired by his devotion and his tenacity.

George does have a divine spark. He still wants to make a difference, he still wants to give, to build and to heal. But the fire that might have raged from his ember has become dampened by the wet blanket of frustration.

Successful Living: A Beloved Canadian Columnist Lives Up to Her Billing
NOVEMBER 1994

Someone who continues to fan sparks wherever she goes is Doris Clark, whom a lot of Canadians met in the early '60s through her column "Successful Living," a popular feature in many daily newspapers across Canada, the United States and Bermuda.

With a Master's degree in social work, she answered "Dear Doris" questions about living and loving and trying to cope with all sorts of personal problems. At that time I was leading a large group of teenagers in a program called Hi-C at a local United Church. Very often at our meetings her name would come up. Someone in the group might have written to her or another had read her column and either agreed or disagreed with her proffered wisdom. When I was asked to find a guest speaker for a conference-wide Hi-C rally, I timidly approached her. She accepted the invitation with alacrity and over 100 teenagers were thrilled and inspired, not just by her talk but with her willingness to answer questions and give individual counselling.

As so often happens over the years, we lost touch, and only recently have I found out about another side to this remarkable woman. In December of last year the Montreal *Gazette* carried a story by Doris called "Getting by in the Dirty Thirties." In it, she told about her experience in the Depression years as a dispenser of "relief" through the Emergency Unemployed Relief Committee of that city. In cooperation with the Protestant Employment Bureau, a morale-boosting contest was launched for homemakers. Notices were posted inviting wives of families on relief to send in ideas on how they used their welfare vouchers; how the grocery list was made up; what the weekly menus were, and what the family's favourite recipes were. First prize was $5, second was $3 and third was $1. The result was a booklet called *How We Do It*. It became very popular with families trying to stretch what little they had in hard times.

She has not been idle in the intervening 60 years. Back in 1970, she and her sister Pearl set up the first retirement planning courses in Hamilton at Mohawk College. Two years ago, she was named Woman of the Year in Communications. Now she has decided that there are many people today who could benefit from the suggestions of earlier unemployed people and has republished her *How We Do It* booklet.

The successful re-release of Doris's book suggests her communications skills are still top-notch. Since the Canadian Press picked up the story, there has been a demand for copies from readers saying, "We need all the help we can get," and "This is a wonderful thing you are doing." Community organizations want it for what it can do to help budget-conscious families. History teachers studying the Depression have also written for it.

This last bit of information comes from Doris herself, who wrote me recently to fill me in on her life since our meeting at the Hi-C rally so long ago. She was prompted to get in touch when she read my column about the difficulty of raising charity money in hard times. She said, "My project may not be a money maker, but it is a money saver."

She also told me her name was now Doris Ludwig. "I joined forces, as it were, with Robert Ludwig, a writer, columnist and public relations man who lived in Vancouver. We were married in 1991. I persuaded him to desert his beloved West Coast and come here to live with me in Hamilton. We are now enjoying working together, being, as Bob says, 'too young to retire.'"

Doris is 86, Bob is 84.

While Doris Clark reached out to millions, May Lemke reached out to one person and wrought her own private miracle.

A Miracle of Human Faith
DECEMBER 1995

May and Joe Lemke lived in a small cottage on Pewaukee Lake, Wisconsin. One day in 1952, a nurse from a Milwaukee hospital told May about a helpless six-month-old baby abandoned to the hospital's care. The parents did not want him and all the hospital knew was that his name was Leslie. After hearing of the baby's condition, May insisted on seeing him.

"He looked like a withered little piece of humanity," she told me. "Gaping eyes, a poor little thing shrivelled up in a ball, so skinny, so thin."

He was almost dead when discovered, with eyes that would not open and so infected they were surgically removed to save what life remained. The doctors then diagnosed severe cerebral palsy with no noticeable mental function. May asked to take the baby home. Since nothing could be done for him at the hospital, her request was granted. "The doctors said they couldn't do anything. They said, 'He's gonna die.'"

But May said, "Oh, shut up. He ain't gonna die. Nothing ever dies that comes to me."

May took the baby home. "There was no movement on his part at all. I would have to put food into his mouth and push it down his throat with my finger. He made no sound, no noise, no nothing. He just lay there like a piece of fluff. In about a year's time he started to suck and chew on his own."

It was about seven years before any real progress was noted — seven years of constant caring, working, training and love. "I had a leather belt with two loops on it so his little hands could go through and I would kind of drag him along behind me trying to teach him to walk. But all he would do is flop." The hours, days, weeks and years went by as they waited for some response. No movement, no emotion, no sound. The only noticeable change was that the baby was growing into a boy.

"I had a fence built on the edge of the property and I would prop Leslie up against it so he could get some fresh air. One day he showed the first sign of movement. Then weeks later he finally pulled himself up on the fence and stood there hanging on. He was 12 years old." Three years later, Leslie took his first steps still clinging to the fence. He could not stand alone and he had never spoken a word.

When Leslie was 16, May's biggest miracle took place. "Joe and I had gone to bed and were asleep. It was about three in the morning. I woke up and said to Joe, 'Hey, where's that music coming from?' I asked Joe if he had left the television set on, but he said no. So I got up and walked down the hall in the dark. And there was Leslie. He was playing the piano. I threw myself down on the floor and said, 'Oh my God. Thank you, thank you. Thank you, dear Creator. You've really made a miracle this time.'"

Not only was Leslie playing, he was playing Tchaikovsky's Piano Concerto no. 1. In the days and weeks that followed, he could hardly be taken away from the keyboard. A flood of tunes came pouring out: ragtime, show tunes, marches, hymns, classical music and obscure old English tunes that May had crooned to him when he was still a baby. Every tune the child had heard from his mother or from the radio, records or television was etched in his brain and could somehow be transformed by his fingers into a fine piano performance. Hands that could not hold a cup or pencil flew with dexterity and sensitivity to fill the tiny cottage with music.

When my program with the Lemkes was broadcast we included explanations by medical scientists about Leslie's condition, which at the time they called "idiot savantism." Today, thankfully, they have dropped the first word. I, however, define it as May's Miracle.

While I find May's private courage deeply inspiring, I am also profoundly affected by the highly public acts of bravery by men like Ernest Harrison.

Honesty is Never Heresy
JUNE 1996

Ernest was no stranger to headlines. In the '60s he was denounced in newspapers, profiled in magazines, criticized on radio and TV talk shows and damned from pulpits throughout Canada and the United States. While his name gradually faded from the headlines, the controversy was not forgotten and was briefly summed up in the headline of his obituary: "Ernest Harrison raised Anglican ire."

I felt I knew him before I met him and certainly before he became my father in-law. I became involved with the communications departments of the Anglican, Roman Catholic and United Churches around the same time as he began "raising ire." My knowledge of religion was slight, to say the least. To get up to speed for my new career, I began cramming on the literature of the day. Fortunately, there was plenty around: Bishop Robinson's *Honest to God*, Harvey Cox's *Secular City*, Pierre Berton's *The Comfortable Pew* (which Ernest had commissioned him to write) and, of course, Ernest's own *Let God Go Free* and *A Church Without God*.

In *A Church Without God*, Ernest examined such taboo subjects as the sex life of Jesus. He said it was doubtful Jesus himself believed in God, suggested that the Gospel account of the Resurrection was unbelievable, and argued that love, not law, is the only absolute in human nature.

I knew that the Anglican Church had reeled from his

criticism and had forced his expulsion. *Heretic* was the word used by many of the church officials and a surprising number of colleagues. Years later the Anglican Church realized its stupidity and offered him back his clerical licence. By this time he was rattling other cages. As a professor of English, he was urging young minds to explore the contradictions, understand the nuances and discover the real meaning in great literature and poetry. After his retirement, he edited books for many Canadian authors — including me.

As a young man, Ernest had wanted to be a social worker, but quickly realized that in Liverpool the best way to help was to become a minister. He earned some scholarships to Oxford but paid much of his way by playing the organ in movie houses. Canada beckoned, and with his doctor wife, Anis, he served parishes in and around Quebec City before the call came from Anglican Church House in Toronto. He was made general-secretary of the Board of Religious Education, where his writing and language skills transformed a moribund church-school curriculum. He also became a successful mystery writer, penning short stories for *Ellery Queen* magazine.

He loved words and, because he knew their power, was scrupulous in their use. A few months before his death I mentioned a book title that used an unfamiliar word. He was like a kid with a new toy, scurrying through his many dictionaries and encyclopedias to discover the precise meaning. It made his day.

As we were assembling for his funeral in April, a
mourner was approached and asked, "Will you be sitting
with the family or the friends of Mr. Harrison?" He replied,
"I never met the man, but what he wrote and what he stood
for had a tremendous effect on my entire life. I just want
to pay my respects."

I believe he affected everyone's life with whom he had
contact. To spend five minutes in his company was to come
away more knowledgeable and more aware of the world
than you were before. He was not a cynic nor a sceptic. He
merely challenged you to open your mind to other possibilities. Whether the topic was music, sports, theatre, politics, theology or any other subject, he had an opinion and
demanded yours.

I was struck by two other comments I overheard at the
small memorial service that followed his funeral. One long-
time friend of Ernest's said, "The church was certainly
precipitous in kicking him out. If he was to write the same
today, no one would blink an eye." A clergyman present
replied, "I'm not so sure. I think the church has slipped
back into its comfortable pew, and we don't have an Ernest
today to blow away the cobwebs. His voice is needed now
more than ever."

I had the honour of being part of his life for over 20
years. It was a heady, fulfilling and cherished experience.
He was no heretic. He was the honest man Diogenes was
hoping to find.

2

A HAPPIER TIME

"We are becoming the servants in thought, as in action, of the machine we have created to serve us."

— JOHN KENNETH GALBRAITH,
THE NEW INDUSTRIAL STATE

Timely Advice for a Society on the Run
OCTOBER 1990

Sometimes I wonder what all the rush is about. We are a society obsessed with time. Our lives revolve around schedules we either meet with great difficulty or miss with feelings of frustration and guilt. A traffic jam, after all, is really just a bunch of people hurrying to get somewhere.

They are cutting down the beautiful old maple trees along my winding country lane in order to straighten and widen the road so that we can get from Point A to Point B five minutes sooner. From microwave ovens to no-iron shirts, we save time. Why? To relax? To enjoy those captured moments? No! To work harder, go faster and save more time.

When most of the world lived in an agrarian society, the changing seasons set our schedule. We did what had to be done according to the weather, not the clock. Craftspeople worked by the job, not the hour. When a task was finished, you stopped because it was done to your satisfaction, not because the five-o'clock whistle blew.

In a 1748 publication entitled *Advice to a Young Tradesman*, Benjamin Franklin wrote these immortal words, "Remember time is money." That concept, plus the emergence of the factory, seemed to start it all. With production lines and profit margins dependent on speed, we became slaves to the clock.

It's interesting to note that in the 1700s the church got involved in the issue, although not out of concern for money. The church said that usury was selling time, and time belonged to God. Well, the church lost that one, as anyone who has borrowed money lately well knows.

Today, time has been organized to a degree that defies understanding. The pulse beat of a computer is the nanosecond — one billionth of a second. This of course speeds up the flow of work. The average good typist used to do 30,000 keystrokes an hour; now the average video display terminal operator can handle 80,000 or more. While this allows us to cope with more details, it also gives us more details with which to cope.

There are businesses now offering time-management seminars so that you and your company can learn to shave off extra minutes. By the way, many of those businesses also offer seminars on how to manage stress, which has become a common modern affliction, alongside the obsession with saving time.

We've also managed, somehow, to reverse a natural order in life. When we are young, healthy and burning up with energy, we sit for hours in treetops inspecting a bird's nest or lie flat on our backs in the grass watching the clouds unfold. When we get older, become overweight and hypertense, we run through airports carrying heavy suitcases, talk on cellular phones while dodging traffic and eat power lunches during business meetings, all for the sake of cramming every precious moment with profitable action.

I used to enjoy the impromptu conversations that would spring up with total strangers on planes and trains. Now the laptop computer has replaced social intercourse and manners. Telephones are now available in business class, so that from 30,000 feet up and hundreds of miles away you can reach out and touch someone at the office to let them know what time zone you are in.

The idea that everything should be accomplished as fast as possible, and that work is of value only for how much it produces, is a societal view that hardly anyone questions. Time saving has become an addiction, a drug. I suppose there is no point in suggesting that we slow down and smell the flowers, because at this very moment there is likely someone inventing a machine that will smell them for us.

What if the time we save cannot be savoured? What if we save an hour but lose the day? When we take time to think about it, the important things in life are timeless.

Taking Work Home and Keeping It There
MARCH 1993

A visitor from the city once asked an old farmer, "What time do you go to work in the morning?"

The farmer answered, "I don't go to work. I wake up surrounded by it."

This could be said of an increasing number of people who have opted to give up the daily round trip to the workplace and, instead, make their living at home. It is something I have been doing for many years.

When I first signed on with CBC-TV back in the 1960s, part of my contract guaranteed an office at its Bay Street headquarters. Since most of the filming was done on location or in a studio, I rarely had the time or predilection to sit in an office. Gradually, it became a depository for old programs, scripts, filing cabinets, a copy machine, research books and a temporary shelter for part-time employees. After a while, the only thing of mine in the office was an in-box from which I would collect my mail from time to time. Finally even my letters were bundled and sent to my home, where I answered them — first in longhand from my seat at the kitchen table, later with elegant sheets from my laser printer.

My home is now my office and I wouldn't have it any other way. My desk is still an old kitchen table, now covered with computer, printer, fax machine, copier, tape-recorder, telephone answering system, microphones and speakers. There is no such thing as commuter trains, rush-hour traffic or parking problems. I can wear jeans, sneakers or my pyjamas if I wish. Shaving is optional.

I live in the country, so if I hit a writer's block or feel the need for inspiration I go for a walk over the fields and commune with nature. I can make myself a snack any time I wish or stretch out on the couch for a nap. Letters are sent and received by way of my rural mailbox and a courier service comes to the door for larger items. I am an early riser and, since my office is always open, can get a lot of chores done before breakfast.

I realize not everyone can work at home, but more and more people are finding ways to do so. Accountants, editors, fashion designers, caterers and management consultants have been featured in recent magazine articles about the growing number of Canadians who have joined the home workforce. A lawyer with a large Toronto firm has arranged to make the trek into the city only two days a week. Other families are using this creative way of balancing career and home. Both father and mother work but rarely, if ever, on the same day. They are then able to look after their children, desirable in and of itself, and save the cost of daycare outside the home. It is also a tremendous boon to the single-parent family where the financial pinch and emotional strain are much greater.

Some companies are reporting significant savings by cutting down on office costs and are experiencing greater productivity as their employees discover the joy of a freer lifestyle. It seems to me the environment must surely benefit from fewer car exhausts and traffic congestion.

However, there are likely those who enjoy getting away from the house every day. Perhaps they need the social fix of the water cooler chat or the power lunch. For me, a conference call is preferable to those interminable and often unnecessary meetings in the boardroom. I like being at home when people drop by. I'm available for childcare if my grandchildren or the neighbour kids need a watchful eye. I don't have to take time off to wait for the TV repair person.

My wife enjoys me working at home. She can't. She's a teacher and has to go where the students are. But she likes the idea of having her weekends free since I can do the laundry any time of the day and look after the banking or grocery shopping at my convenience.

Best of all, when she returns from her workplace she can relax in the knowledge that supper has already been started and that the evening belongs to us.

If there is one drawback to working at home, it's the volume of unsolicited mail that ends up in my in-box here at the farm.

Resorting to Gimmick to Get Donations
SEPTEMBER 1994

I know it's not easy being a fundraiser in a recession. Economists tell us we are not in a recession and that even using the word is counter-productive, but when I continue to meet people whose vocations have entirely disappeared, or who can't make their next mortgage payment or are on their way to the food bank, I don't believe the word is nearly strong enough.

No matter what we call these uncertain times, they are typified by an increasing need for charity dollars amid a shrinking number of benefactors. Every day of the week, our mailbox contains several letters addressed to me or my wife pleading for money. I'm sure we must be on the mailing list of every charity in Canada and several in other countries. Around suppertime, the telephone calls begin. These petitioners would prefer we give them our credit card number or, preferably, access to our savings account for "easy, automatic, monthly withdrawals."

While these requests border on harassment, I am not complaining. I know the need is great. I am aware that hundreds of worthwhile organizations have their backs to the wall as the result of our crippled economy and shrinking government aid. The simple fact is we can't support them all, so, like thousands of other Canadians, we have had to sit down and make a list of where we would like our donations to go and which agencies will be told, "Sorry, no."

As anyone who suffers from a public recognition factor can testify, the appeals for personal involvement have become overwhelming. Anything to raise a buck is requested: after-dinner speeches, celebrity banquets, articles of personal clothing for auction, signed books or photographs for sale, published endorsements and honorary chairmanships. Once again, because of the tremendous increase in requests, the word no has to be used more often.

It is only natural, I guess, that as the competition for the charity dollar intensifies, new and innovative means of extraction must be found.

A self-supporting symphony orchestra in Toronto stages Black-tie Bingo. Celebrity callers catch the bouncing balls and call out the numbers to a well-dressed audience who have paid $50 each for their bingo cards. It's a painless way to give and have fun at the same time.

Children and their desperately poor mothers in Bahia, Brazil, hand-cast and hand-paint little ceramic angels that are sent to anyone who contributes to a fund designed to relieve some of the misery in their ghetto hovels. The project is sponsored by the Weaver Institute, a humanistic and educational charity in Vancouver.

Collective Kitchens in Belleville, Ontario, teaches families cooking skills and proper nutrition. I have been asked to be the "non-speaker" at their "non-dinner" dinner. Rather than a formal dinner with its associated costs, invitations are sent out to people and corporations outlining the concept of this banquet where nobody has to come. You can mail in the cost of your non-meal and get a copy of a short speech that I don't have to give.

I don't particularly care for the word *gimmick*, but hey, if it works, use it. There must be dozens of gimmicks successfully used across this country to raise money for worthy causes. I'd like to hear about them. Perhaps we can share them with others who are struggling to make a difference in this country or around the world.

While I have sympathy for charities that are forced to be aggressive with their solicitations, I have no patience for the advertising material that ends up in my mailbox.

Coming Soon to a Mailbox Near You:
Catalogue Wars

FEBRUARY 1994

I can't help recalling what a joy it used to be to see the mail person come down the street. How eagerly we would rush out to the box in anticipation of a friendly letter, a greeting card, a parcel or that long-awaited cheque. How disappointing when our door was passed and our box was empty.

For those of us who have lived most of our lives in the country, where mailboxes are often a long walk from the house, it was always a delight to see the raised red flag that indicated a pleasant contact with the world beyond. These days, that pleasure has been somewhat dulled.

It's amazing what is regularly being dumped in our rusty old box. Rarely do we get a personal letter. Most of our friends and relatives object to the high cost of postage and find a regular telephone call cheaper and easier. Many people who used to write long, newsy letters now correspond by fax machine and modem. While this has made communication faster, more efficient and available 24 hours a day, it lacks that certain intimacy found on the handwritten page. Bills still arrive, of course, but even they discourage a mailed response, stating that the account may be paid at any bank or by phoning in with a credit card number.

It's been a long time since I received an envelope with "S.W.A.K." (sealed with a kiss) printed boldly on the back. What I do receive are sales flyers by the hundreds advising me of specials to be had on every product imaginable. Packages of discount coupons are so numerous, I can't possibly read them all, let alone use them. Brochures arrive every morning telling of once-in-a-lifetime real-estate opportunities in Florida, romantic vacations in Aruba or exercise machines guaranteed to firm up my thighs.

I've also noticed that if you send money in aid of one charity you suddenly are deluged with requests from 50 others asking for donations to save this, get rid of that or help harangue your MP about something else.

The greatest increase in the material weighing down my mail carrier's car and jamming my mailbox comes from catalogues. Where we used to receive a couple each year from old firms like Eaton's or Canadian Tire, we now are getting half a dozen each week from companies that have obviously found this to be an effective way to move merchandise.

At first glance, the American catalogues are very seductive with their easy ordering plans and low prices. However, when you add on the tariff, applicable sales taxes plus shipping and handling costs, your purchase becomes less of a bargain. I'm also not keen on giving my credit card number over the phone. And while it's fun flipping through these catalogues, looking at the pretty pictures and comparing prices, I still prefer visiting an actual store where I can see and feel the merchandise.

Apparently we are just at the beginning of a catalogue war between American and Canadian companies. The U.S. market has become saturated, and while some, like the giant Sears Roebuck & Co., have gone out of business, others such as L.L. Bean, Eddie Bauer, J. Crew and Lands' End have turned their focus on Canada.

There are also a large number of smaller firms with specialty catalogues featuring food, jewellery, electronics or Native American crafts. One that comes to our house regularly advertises slippers with battery-operated lights in the toes so you can see your way to the bathroom in the dark.

Canadian companies are preparing to meet the competition head on. Sears Canada recently opened a $180-million catalogue service centre in Belleville, Ontario, and introduced a toll-free telephone ordering system. Market analysts forecast a boom in direct-mail companies in this country as we try to stave off the American invasion.

It seems certain that, as this mode of marketing increases, it will be a long time before we ever have to experience an empty mailbox.

Just as we seem to have lost the art of writing personal letters, it seems to me we have also lost our facility for witty and frank conversation.

Learning the Art of Saying the Right Thing

JUNE 1991

I realized long ago that I would never have the mental agility to create the *bons mots* of a Dorothy Parker, Fred Allen or Malcolm Muggeridge when commenting on social or political issues — or even the sagacity of a Yogi Berra, whose homespun bloopers are a joy to the ear. I would have to be satisfied to come up with the appropriate words to say to people in normal conversation, especially when you meet someone who is going through a troubled period in life.

I imagine there are a lot of people who, like me, always seem to offer tongue-tied clichés as an expression of concern or sympathy. How many times, standing with a grieving relative beside a casket, have you said something like, "My, she looks so natural"? Then you bite your tongue because, of course, she doesn't look natural at all. It's small consolation when one is in pain to hear the advice, "This too shall pass." Telling a friend who is going through a marriage break-up "Someday you'll look back on this and laugh" garners the contempt the remark deserves.

A few weeks ago I went to see my old friend Sam, who was recovering from a serious heart operation. I wasn't looking forward to the visit because I knew he'd had a very rough time and was feeling quite depressed. During the drive there, I was rehearsing all the things I felt I could safely say. When I arrived in his room I began by asking, "How are you feeling?"

"I'm feeling terrible" was his reply.

"Are you in pain?" I asked.

"The only pain," he said, "are the pains in the butt who come in here trying to cheer me up. Roy, you wouldn't believe some of the stupid things they say. They start out with 'You look wonderful.' I look like something the cat dragged in. I'm thin, pale and tired.

"Nobody will mention my heart," he said. "They'll say anything except the H-word. But it was one heck of an exciting operation and I'd love to tell someone about it. But if I even mention it, then they start talking about how lucky I am, that the situation isn't nearly as bad as what a friend of theirs had been through. Then there are the ones who say, 'I know just how you feel.' They're nuts. Unless they've had a triple bypass they haven't the foggiest notion how I feel."

"You know, Sam," I said, "people are only trying to be kind."

"Kind!" he snorted. "They're driving me up the wall. And the ones who really bug me are those who tell me about some wonderful doctor who just does miracles. My doctor did a great job.

"The thing is, I had an operation, I am not senile. Why can't visitors in hospital rooms carry on normal conversations? I'd like to talk about what is going on in the world."

"Well, Sam," I said. "why don't you take the initiative

and tell them just what you've told me? Let them know you've heard all the clichés and are tired of them."

A couple of days ago, I heard Sam was feeling somewhat better, so I phoned his room and was delighted when he answered me so cheerfully. "I'm doing just fine," he said, "and all because I took your advice. I had a nurse type out a list of dos and don'ts, things I didn't want to hear and subjects I didn't want to talk about. I had her tape the list to the foot of the bed. It's amazing the topics I've been discussing. I didn't know some of my friends were so smart. Thanks for the suggestion."

Apparently, this was one time I did manage to say something right.

This past summer, the whole Bonisteel family managed to do something right.

The Reunion
OCTOBER 1996

There's an old song that says, "The things we did last summer, I'll remember all winter long." Isn't it true? With the possible exception of Christmas, the summer holiday season brings families together more intensely than any other time. For me, these crisp autumnal days are warmed with gentle memories of the weeks just past.

Nothing particular happened. No long trips or tourist excursions. Just a melding of pleasant days and nights where friends and relatives drifted in and out of my life. A lot of joyous hello hugging and regretful goodbye kissing.

I live on a farm in a community where people never make appointments or even call in advance. The first indication that you may have to stretch the soup or make up an extra bed is when you hear the crunch of car tires in the laneway. Most visitors come laden with extra food, drink and sleeping bags.

One long weekend turned into a family reunion. Bonisteels I thought had died showed up. Children I didn't know existed were introduced. Comments such as "My, you have grown," "You certainly have your mother's eyes" and "Whatever happened to cousin Bessie?" filled the air. Some were complete strangers, since a lot of families on vacation these days seem to take along their children's school chums or neighbour friends, to say nothing of their cats and dogs.

Psychologists tell us that summer is a particularly stressful time for parents. Most of the year is spent adhering to a predictable agenda. Kids spend their required hours at school and their weekends in organized sports or doing homework. Parents are tied to a working schedule and there are few unaccounted hours. The holiday season changes all that. Families are pushed together for weeks at a time in cars, motels, campsites and cottages. Travel is costly and drains the budget. Tempers fray. Mom and Dad are asking, "Can we afford the price of Marineland?" Kids are demanding, "How soon do we get there?"

With so many broken relationships today, there is the added trauma for children who have to divide their holiday time between divorced spouses. For a lot of kids, their whole summer becomes a blur of estranged parents, defunct grandparents and strange siblings. Often you can see them at the airport in July or August, which has become known in the airline industry as the "UM" (unaccompanied minor) travel season, being shuttled to and fro.

I was away from home for only one week this year. My wife and I have an old cottage in a secluded cove along a crystal-clear Quebec river. On one side is a white sand beach, on the other towering pines that whisper you to sleep at night. No television, no fax machine, no alarm clock. Just books, jigsaw puzzles, canoes and each evening, a sunset that seems to be competing with the previous one. When we met our neighbours there, the talk was of loons, wildflowers, recipes for spaghetti sauce and big fish that never seem to get caught. The word *separatist* was in no one's lexicon.

Back on the farm, the sunsets were followed by bonfires. One night, there must have been close to 50 people sitting in a circle staring at the flames, teary-eyed from the smoke, telling jokes, singing songs, spinning ghost tales and toasting marshmallows. Do people eat those things any other time of year? I vowed that if I heard "B-I-N-G-O Was His Name" one more time, I would scream. However, I do get as scared as my grandchildren when my daughter-in-law tells, once again, the frightening Bloody Claw story.

So if I had to answer that perennial question asked by teachers when school resumes, "What did you do on your summer vacation?" the answer would likely be: I put on a little weight from too much potato salad; learned how to dance the delightful macarena; saw my first yellow-bellied sapsucker; became rather good at playing horseshoes, and rediscovered the overwhelming joy of sharing the love of family and friends.

A Society Where Death Is Deceitful
FEBRUARY 1992

The older one gets, the more funerals one should expect to attend. That obvious fact, however, doesn't make the experience any better. I went to my first one when I was ten, my most recent was a few weeks ago. I shall probably go to several more before I attend my own. And each time I go to pay my final respects to someone, I find that the whole process, including death itself, is becoming more and more like a bad farce. Human beings, it is said, are the only animals that know they are going to die. I think we have borne that privileged information with uneven grace.

I've been in hospital rooms where doctors have told

dying patients, "We're going to have you out of here in no time." They didn't have the courage to mention it would be in a hearse. I've been at funerals where the priest kept calling the deceased by the wrong name. I was at a service last year where the minister tried to convert all the mourners to his particular faith. I've seen relatives on the verge of fisticuffs trying to arrange wakes.

These days, most of us die in hospitals without the benefits of the liturgies that attend the natural event in cultures that accept death as more of a human fact. Modern technology and advances in medicine have made it possible to maintain threatened life to an incredible degree. We now have the capacity to sustain vital functions by extraordinary, artificial means or to make a composite body by transplantation of organs.

I remember the Hilaire Belloc poem:

> Of old when men lay sick and sorely tried,
> The doctor gave them physic and they died.
> But here's a happier age, for now we know,
> Both how to make men sick, and keep them so.

Death should be faced long before it happens. In 1987 a Canadian Medical Association study on care for seniors, conducted by a committee led by palliative care booster Dr. Dorothy Ley, said that one goal of the health-care system should be to enrich the lives of older people rather than prolonging life for its own sake.

She said, "Physicians should be concerned about how their patients die, rather than when they die." In an interview last year she put it this way. "The public is saying, I don't want to die in a hospital with tubes in this end and out that end ... where no one is interested in me, where I'm just a disease in a bed."

Three years ago at a hospital seminar on palliative care, David Roy of the Centre for Bioethics in Montreal spoke strongly against giving dying people drugs instead of helping them face their anxiety about death. He said that to use chemicals to control the behaviour of the dying because of fear or lack of time was to "treat humans the way we would want to treat our pets."

Dying in our society is marked by deceit. Everything can be addressed except the important fact of impending death. Then, when the unmentionable happens, the deceit goes on as the embalmer embarks on the post-mortem cosmetics to make the dead person look alive. The mourners continue the farce by reciting their lines about "how well the person looks." Ministers often join in by claiming the dear departed is "only sleeping."

How do we clear this smokescreen of deceit from such a natural act? Admitting our own mortality would be a start. Discussing it with our family and friends would be a kind and loving act.

They say that once you're born, the only sure things are death and taxes. Our health-care system has managed to turn both birth and death into cold, mechanical experiences. I suppose we can take some comfort in the fact that as yet they haven't developed surgical means for extracting taxes.

Seat Belts Fastened on a Flight to Boredom
MARCH 1991

In the early '60s, I took my first airplane trip from Toronto to Vancouver. I remember it with great clarity. Everything I had been told about this immensely sprawling country could not compare to actually seeing its face. I was blessed with a window seat and my nose was nearly flattened before we reached the Manitoba border.

What beauty, what texture — the colours, shapes and shadows spilled out below like an artist's canvas coming to life. I knew Saskatchewan and Alberta were big but it wasn't until I saw the swirling rows of yellow grain pushing the brown ribs of ploughed earth into seeming infinity that I understood how vast the Prairies actually were. Using the flight map provided by the airline, we followed our progress by spotting the Athabasca and Bow Rivers far below.

The pilot, playing master of ceremonies, seemed as excited as the passengers. "And now, ladies and gentlemen ... just appearing on the horizon ... the foothills, to be followed in a minute by the fabulous Rockies." Then came the spectacular sweep over the Pacific with the rolling waves sending glints of sunlight back to my window.

I have made that same flight many times, and even when travel-exhausted or in low spirits I have felt restored and uplifted by seeing this magnificent country unfold below me.

I made the trip again last month. This time I saw no fields, lakes, rivers or mountains. You aren't allowed to any more. As you fly across Canada, you can read, work on your personal computer or do crossword puzzles, but you can't look out the window.

On take-off right after you are told to stow your luggage in the overhead racks, fasten your seat belt and reminded not to smoke, the next command is, "Please direct your attention to the screen at the front of your cabin. In just a moment we will be presenting a short film outlining the safety features of this aircraft. Following this will be a shopper's guide of items available for purchase from your flight attendants. And then, our feature film. Today we are presenting *Kindergarten Cop* starring Arnold Schwarzenegger. Those of you with window seats, please lower the blinds so that we may all enjoy these entertainment features."

You can squint at feature films plus commercial and safety messages, you can eat steak dinners and booze it up until you are silly. You can count the hairs on the head of the person sitting in front of you, but you can't peer down at the winding St. Lawrence, marvel at the craggy coast of Nova Scotia or the red sand of Prince Edward Island.

You can't even talk to the people next to you. Their

ears are plugged with plastic headphones. When the window blind was allowed to be up, your seat-mate would lean over and "ooh" and "aah" along with you. There was no ice-breaker as effective as two bodies pressed together viewing the grandeur of the Gaspé Peninsula. Now, with eyes transfixed on a blurry screen and with tinny static roaring in our ears, we hurtle across the sky in our solitary cocoons, immune to contact with the living world.

For that first Toronto–Vancouver trip I paid $175 return. It was worth a million. Last month I paid $1,498 for the same flight, and it wasn't worth a nickel.

One thing that will always be worth its weight in gold is the input of a good editor.

The Deft Human Hand of the Editor
JUNE 1994

In the Tennessee Williams play *A Streetcar Named Desire*, Blanche Dubois reflects, "I have always depended on the kindness of strangers." Most writers would paraphrase that remark, "I've always depended on the kindness of editors." Or at least on their expertise.

As a cub newspaper reporter in the '50s, I had been writing for several months happily seeing my words in black and white exactly as they had been pounded out on my old Underwood. Then the newspaper changed editors. Suddenly, my copy was being sent back corrected, blue-pencilled and altered beyond recognition.

Pat Quinn was an old-time newspaper man who simply would not abide a poorly constructed sentence, a misspelled word or a dangling participle. Sometimes he carried his passion for proper word usage to extremes. Once, when I submitted a short news item about a meeting of the local Ladies' Aid Society, he asked me how many in the group were titled or the wives of lords. When I answered none, he promptly rechristened them, in print, the Women's Aid Society.

In radio, not only did my news editor vet every item before airing but he listened intently for mispronunciations and improper inflections. Television employs a host of editors to check scripts and tidy up rambling interviews by cutting film and electronically editing tape for succinct and intelligible productions. The editor makes everyone look good.

Book publishers employ their own editors to scrupulously check every word. Sometimes even that is not enough. When my first book came out, my father-in-law, an author and former English professor, discovered 50 errors. Needless to say, before he died I submitted every book manuscript to him before publication.

I have been thinking about the role of editors lately because of something I have noticed in the newspapers and magazines arriving in my home. Reporters and columnists whom I have enjoyed over the years appear word-sloppy and difficult to comprehend. I find myself reading a paragraph over and over to discover the meaning. Spelling and grammar mistakes are rampant.

I now realize that these writers are as good as they ever were. It's just that now they are not being properly edited. At least by a human being. Increasingly publishers are moving to reduce costs by turning to computer pagination, wherein newspaper or magazine pages are designed on a computer screen. In the days when pages destined for the giant presses were composed of metal, the process was known as typesetting. Later, when hot lead was replaced by wax-covered strips of photosensitive paper, the art of putting type on a page was called paste-up. Publishers like pagination because it allows them to lay off those union-prone paste-up crews in the back shop and assign the job of page layout to the editors.

Problem is, editing is a thinking game. The publishing industry has yet to come up with technology that makes people think faster, or better. Yet editors who once devoted all their energy to whipping prose into shape are now spending much of their time as electronic paste-up artists, nudging columns into place on a computer monitor. And publishers certainly haven't been hiring more editors.

While computers may be equipped with spelling checkers, they are only a minor aid to harried editors. If a word exists, the spell-checker usually accepts it. For example, most spell-checking software gives this sentence the green light: "I send a ladder two me life in all the weigh I dripped it." An alert human editor could easily see that this isn't the sought-after phrase.

Most of our schools are now being equipped with computers and students are urged to run their essays and assignments through the spell-checker for accuracy. It may help tidy up their writing but it will not by itself teach them the rudiments of spelling or grammar or instil a sense of proper word usage.

Until my computer is able to proofread with the acquired knowledge and sensitivity of the late Pat Quinn or my father-in-law, I will continue to proclaim that an editor is a writer's best friend.

That way, I can be assured that every sentence that appears here will be prefect.

One fact that we can't edit out of our lives is that alienation, withdrawal, anxiety, depression and tension seem to be the hallmarks of modern society.

To Do Our Jobs Well, We Have to Stay Well
MARCH 1995

The Canadian Mental Health Association describes the situation as critical. The group claims that half the hospital

beds in Canada are occupied by the mentally or emotion-
ally ill. One-third of the population has suffered some temporary disability because of emotional problems. Mental
disorders such as anxiety are a factor in 50 per cent of the
cases seen in general practice. Suicide is now the second
most frequent cause of death among Canadians between
the ages of 15 and 30.

I found these statistics startling, yet, when I talked
with members of the medical profession, and with friends
who have had or are having problems, the figures appear
accurate.

Psychiatrists tell us the big offender is the workplace.
American statistics show us that 46 per cent of all workplace disabilities are related to mental health. Sixty to 80
per cent of all workplace accidents have been attributed
to emotional problems, and one-quarter of all medical
claims are made for that reason.

While every area of our workforce is affected, it seems
that health-care, service and factory workers suffer the
most. Those occupations tend to be characterized by
stressful conditions, repetition, shift work and, in the case
of the first two categories, responsibility for other people.
The pattern of breakdown is well documented.

Conditions such as work overload, non-supportive
bosses and colleagues, limited job opportunity, undefined
tasks, rotating work shifts and operating at a machine-set
pace all contribute to a worker's dissatisfaction. In turn,

those factors cause psychological disorders including neu-
roses and depression, irritability, drug abuse, sleep difficulties, and even simpler complaints such as headache and
stomach-ache.

There is also the added pressure of trying to hold on to
a job while others around you are losing theirs. Many people are working extra hours for no extra pay either to
impress the boss or because the boss makes it clear that
if they don't, there are plenty who will.

The health and financial costs of this type of illness to
our society are staggering, and indications are that these
will increase. New technologies in the workplace are shift-
ing the more physically demanding tasks to more mental
and repetitive ones. Working women are particularly vul-
nerable as they face unequal pay rates, fewer job opportunities, less chance for promotion, and the conflict between
the demands of the job and the home.

The employer certainly has a large role to play in seeking a solution to this situation but cannot possibly do it
alone. Governments and labour unions also have a stake
in a healthy workforce. Health-care specialists are indis-
pensable in helping set up clinics or human resources centres in industry. A few years ago in the United States,
General Motors began a wellness program for its 44,000
employees. After it went into effect, absenteeism dropped
by 40 per cent and grievances were cut by 50 per cent.

I also think a big part of any program of this type has

to do with fellow employees. Being aware of the people next to you on the line or in the office or down the hall, paying attention to their concerns or problems and helping if you can but sometimes just learning how to listen can go a long way toward creating a healthy work environment.

Adopting a caring attitude toward our co-workers might very well help with our own emotional well-being.

Alternative Medicine from the Pantry Shelf
JANUARY 1996

I like a good party. I like meeting people and, more to the point, I like good conversation. This season I noticed how much of the party chatter revolved around "alternative medicine." It seemed almost everyone I talked to was involved in some therapy or treatment that did not involve a general practitioner or a pill.

Aromatherapy is one example. This therapy features the use of "essential oils" to promote relaxation and phys-ical healing. These oils are inhaled, massaged into the skin or added to the bath water to stimulate certain glands to release beneficial neurochemicals, according to adherents.

Reflexology, or acupressure, is similar to acupuncture minus the needles. Pressure is applied to points on the body to encourage healing by stimulating nerve cells. Reiki is a method developed in the late nineteenth century by a Japanese Christian minister who was also a Buddhist monk. Reiki practitioners claim to be able to transfer their healing energy to others and effect both physical and emotional healing through touch.

As much as I enjoyed my holiday conversations, I couldn't help but recall a time when our family was practising "alternative medicine" without the label. Our old farm community looked after itself. We seldom had to go to specialists for help or advice. Medical requirements for human or animal were mostly attended to by old remedies that had been passed down for generations. Very often, the nostrum was the same for both.

For simple ailments there was always something on hand to ease the pain. A clove bud stuck in a cavity eased a toothache. An earache felt better when you held a bag of heated salt against it. A warm wet tea bag fastened to your eye overnight made a sty disappear by morning and left your sheets full of tea leaves. A silk stocking around your throat when it was sore, turpentine and brown sugar ingested for worms, iodine applied on cuts, boracic acid for disinfectant and carbolic soap if lice were suspected were all routine treatments.

Colds for every member of the family were inevitable. Working in all kinds of weather, freezing in some rooms of the house and roasting in others, and sleeping two and three to a bed meant that someone was always sneezing or coughing at any given time. Fortunately, catnip or peppermint tea would make you sleep, honey and eucalyptus would soothe the throat, and a sniff from a strange brown bottle on the sideboard would clear out the most stubborn nasal passages. It was many years before I found out the bottle contained stale horse urine and the ammonia fumes did the job.

I have an old recipe book that belonged to my aunt Emma that contains directions for everything from floor paint to wedding cake. One is simply titled "Good Cough Mixture": 2 oz. glycerine, ½ oz. virgin oil of pine ... and 8 oz. pure whisky.

I don't know if Aunt Emma ever used this remedy or not. I do know she was 97 when she died and she always seemed *very* happy.

One of the best things about home medicine is that it prevents trips to the store, which aren't as much fun as they used to be.

Unsatisfied Consumers
SEPTEMBER 1991

Many reasons are being given for current business failures, including the recession, free trade, high taxes and foreign competition. While all of these certainly contribute to the current economic malaise, I'm wondering if there is not another factor involved — one called customer dissatisfaction.

As we put the brakes on our spending habits because of leaner wallets, some of us are demanding a return to old-fashioned service and quality merchandise.

I went into a hardware store the other day to buy a sledgehammer; I had some fence to fix at the back of my farm. When I picked one up to take it over to the counter, the hammer head fell off. The clerk, when I found one, said brightly, "No problem. All you have to do is drive a couple of nails in along the side of the handle and it will stay on fine."

"But, I'm paying $32.50 for this," I protested. "Why should I have to repair it before it leaves the store?"

"Okay," he replied, "I'll see if there's one in the back."

He found one in the storeroom that seemed to be in good condition. When I paid for my purchase I casually asked, "By the way, what will you be doing with the other one?"

I believed him when he answered, "I'll sell it to someone who isn't so fussy."

Over the past few years, I have been running into more than the usual number of salespeople with slapdash attitudes toward their products and their customers. I'm sure I'm not the only one who gets lonely in a department store. Whatever happened to the salesperson who used to come up and ask, "Can I help you?"

With computerized inventories not much is kept in stock these days; consequently everything you really want is always on back-order. Or, you'll be told, "We can have it for you by next Tuesday."

When things go on sale you don't get to buy them, you get rain checks. When you finally find a basketful of items you need, you jockey for position in front of the only two cashiers on duty, waiting while they answer the telephone or chat to each other about their adventures from the night before.

It seems to me that one of the joys in life is taking pride in what you do. I think we lost a lot when we went from craftsmanship to simply producing *things*. Now we expect things to fall apart shortly after we buy them. Perhaps the manufacturer knows we'll find it easier to just go out and purchase new ones, rather than go through all the hassles of sending things to be fixed. Returning goods these days is not easy. You are instructed to repack the item in its original carton, which of course you've already tossed out, and send it, not to the local store where you bought it, but to some clearing house in the bowels of Toronto or Montreal, allowing six months for repairs.

It's likely shoddy merchandise that causes shoddy sales attitudes. If you don't like the product, how can you possibly enjoy selling it? Compare a waiter in a restaurant that serves tasty, nourishing creations with the robot-like workers in a fast-food place. Compare the salesperson who obviously enjoys the books sold in a quality shop with the one in the chain bookstore who, when asked "Where can I find Margaret Atwood?" says, " I think she phoned in sick."

I think I'll begin a personal campaign not to go to stores without enough clerks to provide good-quality service, and to report personally every inferior item of merchandise to the store manager with a letter to the manufacturer. I'll also talk to other shoppers in the store or clients in the bank to see if they're happy with the way they've been treated.

I think we have a right to expect more than just being told, "Have a Nice Day."

3

THE WORLD
AROUND US

*"Lost is our old simplicity of times,
The world abounds with laws,
and teems with crimes."*

— ANONYMOUS

Life in Canada's Rural Slow Lane
AUGUST 1994

A friend was trying to coax his aged, housebound father to go for a car ride. "Come on, Dad, you'll enjoy it. How about a ride in the country? When you were a kid you lived in the country."

His father answered, "Son, when I was a kid, everybody lived in the country."

The old man was not far off track. There was a time
when the rural population counted for something in this
nation. They were the backbone of Canadian society. They
provided the fish, meat, milk, grain, fruits and vegetables
that kept our cities alive and healthy. Before our cities
became steel- and glass-walled cocoons, there was a closer
relationship between the town folk and their country
cousins. Even if you lived in the heart of the city you were
likely related to someone who made a living in agriculture,
or you spent the summer on Grandpa's farm, or you enjoyed
a leisurely drive in the open spaces now and again.

Politicians certainly paid attention to the rural vote. The
concerns of the farm constituency were uppermost on the
agenda of any politico who had the faintest hope of holding office. Now, to get the attention of the federal or provincial governments, farmers have to block highways with
hay wagons, circle the parliament buildings with tractors
or manure spreaders, dump oceans of milk or let mountains
of grain rot in the field.

During the Second World War, the farmer was as important as the soldier. The demand for food to stoke the war
machine was immense. In the years that followed, there
were many changes down on the old homestead. Sons and
daughters of families that had farmed for generations left
for the cities where jobs, education and bright lights beckoned. Urban sprawl gobbled up some of the most precious
acreage. Low food prices and technology forced farming

into agribusiness and a reduced need for manual labour. Small local cheese factories, canning companies, grain mills and hundreds of other processing facilities were bought up by food conglomerates and moved to town. The complexion of rural Canada changed.

In the '50s the farm population was around 24 per cent of the total. Now it's less than 4 per cent. Because those of us who live in the country have lost our clout, we tend to be ignored.

I love living in the country. I wouldn't exchange the fresh air, the space, the neighbours, the bond with earth and green for any city penthouse or mansion, yet it's interesting how easily we are taken for granted. It's the small things, like trying to telephone into the city.

When a recorded voice tells us to push the touch-tone button, we have to hang up. Many of us are still on party lines, let alone having buttons to touch. Cable stations find it too expensive to wire us up because our homes are too far apart. National surveys or poll takers don't call us for opinions. Politicians find it inconvenient to knock on our doors. Advertisements about delivering pizza in 30 minutes don't apply here; neither does the advice to call 911 in case of an emergency. We don't have such a number. There is also no movie "playing at a theatre near you."

On the other hand, when we hear your traffic reports, smog alerts and news stories about people being mugged or slaughtered in the streets of the cities, perhaps it's just as well we have become anonymous. Those of us who have opted for the country lane instead of the fast lane should really count our blessings.

The Best View Is from the Sidelines
NOVEMBER 1993

Country life also means the absence of professional sports teams. Perhaps that's why I have never been a very enthusiastic sports fan. While I am sometimes swept up in the national excitement of a Blue Jays World Series quest or the Montreal Canadiens Stanley Cup finals, for the most part, the sports section of my daily paper remains unread. At social gatherings I depend on my wife, Jane, to keep up our end of the conversation when talk turns to John Olerud's batting average or Steffi Graf's tennis ratings. This saves me from embarrassing gaffes. Once when a chap told me he played golf in the low 80s, I assumed he was referring to the temperature.

When I worked in radio, one of my jobs was to read the commercials during the live Junior A hockey broadcasts. This meant travelling to various cities, spending hours in crowded broadcast gondolas high in the rafters of cold arenas. I always took a book to read while the actual game was going on. During one crucial play-off game I peered over the edge of the booth to watch a particularly brilliant shot on goal and our colour commentator announced, "This has to be a most exciting contest. Even Roy is paying attention."

A few years ago, I was asked to speak at a community function in the town where I had attended high school. My former principal, a man now in his eighties, made the introduction. As he spoke at length about my scholastic achievements I began to think he had me confused with someone else, as I was never a more than average student. My suspicions were confirmed when he said, "I always knew he would be a success in life because of his remarkable ability on the gridiron." The fact is I have never worn a football uniform in my life and am still hopelessly confused by the game.

Perhaps an appreciation of sports is genetic. I never saw my parents skate, swim or toss a ball into a basket. Our family's idea of competition was a session of crokinole or a few hands of euchre. A softball game and some three-legged races at the annual Sunday school picnic was about the extent of our athletic prowess.

I suspect my real problem with organized sporting events is that someone has to lose. I find it very difficult to watch the pain in the face of a runner who hits the ribbon a few seconds late or the bloodied countenance of a boxer beaten unconscious in the ring. I dislike the boos from the grandstand when the shortstop misses the ball, and my heart goes out to the racehorse as it limps in last. The conventional wisdom is that sports are good training for life where some people win and some lose. This old bromide is usually touted by the winners.

This past summer I was asked to do the announcing at the opening ceremonies of the Canada Summer Games in Kamloops, B.C. It was a thrilling event as 4,000 young athletes from all ten provinces and two territories surged into the stadium to the cheers and applause of 10,000 spectators. There seemed to be no favourites, as smaller contingents were welcomed as heartily as the large.

For the first time in the history of the games, native traditional sports were featured. Another first was the participation of disabled athletes, such as blind swimmers and wheelchair racers.

In the days that followed, you could see the results of hundreds of hours of practice on the part of the athletes, some as young as 10 and 12. You could also imagine the hard work of coaches and trainers, the sacrifice and encouragement of parents and friends. I'm sure many who watched the 18 different sports wanted their own province to win, but you got the impression they were cheering just as hard for either side. Of course, the individual boy or girl wanted to be successful, but I think the majority were just happy to be there. It was a celebration of personal challenge, a competition in the spirit of fair play, bringing honour to themselves and their country.

As in any contest some left with medals and some with just memories, but in a real sense there were no losers.

That's my idea of good sport.

While I don't much care for the concept of dividing people into winners and losers, I sometimes find myself caught up in anticipating how a sporting event will turn out. Yet what will be, will be. These are good words to keep in mind when we wade through the plethora of predictions made by so-called experts in our society.

Predicting the Future, Ignoring the Present
JANUARY 1993

Every January, our economy, our political future and even our personal lives are dissected, catalogued and projected into the uncharted days that make up the new year.

At the beginning of every year, the media give space and time to astrologers telling us where we and our planet are headed. Their ploy is to use the scatter-gun approach, making hundreds of predictions in the belief that some will be right. Nostradamus, the daddy of pop astrology, did the same thing back in the 1500s, spawning the Jeane Dixons of today. It's vaguely amusing to read what the birth signs say about Charles and Di or Madonna, and it's perfectly harmless as long as we don't start living our own lives according to the position of Pluto.

I guess it's normal to wonder about the future and even to speculate over what it will hold for us. Will the economy improve? Will the free trade deal work? Will I get a job? Can I hold on to the one I have? Will my family enjoy good health this coming year? Some answers will come from our own individual efforts and some are out of our control, but all will be the result of a day-by-day pilgrimage into the future. None will be decided by any one expert.

Why intelligent people in business, medicine, sports or science make definitive statements about the future, I'll never figure out. How must they feel when their prognostications are proven wrong?

American historian Henry Adams (1838–1918) stated, "My figures coincide in fixing 1950 as the year the world must go smash." And Waldeman Kaemfort, editor of *Science America* magazine, said in 1913, "Airplanes will never carry more than five to seven passengers."

I find it interesting to look back at some of the predictions made even in my lifetime:

"Television won't be able to hold on to any market it captures after the first six months. People will soon get tired of staring at a plywood box every night" (Darryl F. Zanuck, film producer, 1946).

"Nuclear-powered vacuum cleaners will be a reality within ten years" (Alex Lewyt, manufacturer, 1955).

"I think there is a world market for about five computers" (Thomas J. Watson, chairman of IBM, 1943).

A young couple told me recently they had no intention of having children because the future of our ecosystem was so bleak.

Should we believe the predictions being made today

for the near future? Irene Hughes, a native American, fore-tells the future through a Japanese spirit guide. She said that February 1993 would see the outbreak of a world-wide nuclear conflict.

Olof Jonsson, a Swedish psychic known for his amazing extrasensory abilities, claimed that by 1995 the internal combustion engine will be outlawed in all major North American cities and that by 2000 there will be no more automobiles.

I can understand the interest in wanting to know the future. Sometimes while reading my morning paper I'll glance at the astrology column to see what is in the cards for Gemini. The only time the prediction seems to come true is when it says I'm going to take a trip or receive a letter. These both happen far too often.

The sad part about believing in forecasters and speculators is the time we lose savouring today. Each hour of our lives is the most valuable, and one of the great joys of living each day at a time is the sweet mystery of the future. My mother used to have a saying that I particularly remember at the onset of a new year. I don't know whether it was original or not but I can't recall hearing anyone else say it. It went like this:

"Yesterday is a cancelled cheque; tomorrow is a promissory note; today is the only cash you have, so spend it wisely."

Don't Put Your Faith in Those Who Predict

MAY 1995

There are a number of people who make a very good living today predicting the future. Some are economists, sociologists or philosophers, lumped under the new rubric "futurists." They write books or magazine articles and hold seminars designed to help us plan our lives or businesses for the years to come. Then there are those who use the stars, planets, historical data, intuition or their own variety of crystal ball to tell us what's ahead. I take some of these people seriously, others I find very entertaining, but there is one area of the prediction business that I find extremely sad: prophesying the end of the world. One wit refers to it as the "Armageddon outta here" syndrome.

Now I see where Jeane Dixon, who has had a better-than-average record of accuracy on social prognostications, says that in 2020 the Antichrist will be revealed and the Battle of Armageddon will take place. Don't believe her.

From the beginning of recorded time we have been told: The End Is Near! In the Apocrypha it was prophesied that the world would end in 1,000 years. As the date drew near, people gave away their property to ensure themselves a place in heaven. On December 31, 999, thousands left their homes and climbed to the top of Mount Zion, where Jesus was supposed to appear. Nothing happened.

During the first half of the sixteenth century, England

swarmed with fortune-tellers and astrologers. February 1, 1524, was chosen as a final day. Twenty thousand people sold their belongings and moved out of their homes. Getting rid of all one's belongings as the final day draws near fulfils the biblical command to "take nothing out of this world." In 1524, the day came and passed. The prophesiers said there had been a slight miscalculation. The end would come in 1624.

I remember in 1953 writing news reports of the Children of Light, a Canadian religious sect based near Vancouver. Their leader announced that January 9, 1954, would mark the end of the world. Faithful converts and their children holed up in a vacant farmhouse singing hymns and waiting. The day came and went.

Jeane Dixon isn't the only one who has set a doomsday date. Some prophets have chosen 1998 for the end, based on their calculations that Christ died in the 1,998th week of his life. Criswell, a psychic prophet, claims that a black rainbow or "magnetic disturbance" will suck the oxygen out of the earth's atmosphere in 1999. Then the planet will race into the sun, incinerating everyone and everything.

In 1976 I noticed in my local paper that a 150-acre farm was for sale a few miles from where I lived. I didn't know the owner that well but I was familiar with the farm. As a boy I had climbed its hills and hiked across its meadows and along its sparkling creeks. There was a large brick farmhouse and a sturdy dairy barn on the property. Mildly interested, I visited the owner, a man in his forties, and asked why he was selling. "Because the world is coming to an end one year from next month. I'm getting rid of all my earthly possessions," he answered. When I enquired about the price, he replied, "Twenty-five thousand dollars."

Considerably more interested, I protested, "But this place is worth five times that."

"I know," he said. "But $25,000 is all I need to live on for one year. We are promised that when Judgement Day comes the wicked will perish and the righteous shall inherit the earth. Not only will I be saved, but I'll likely get my farm back."

I stared at him in astonishment and disbelief. Then I bought his farm.

Pledging to Be Green at Time of Renewal
APRIL 1990

As time marches on, journalists continue to come up against a problem that has always bedevilled them: how to say something fresh about a story that's been around for a couple of thousand years. I was recently reminded of this when a radio producer from Regina called to ask if I would take part in a special Easter broadcast.

This producer developed the idea of tying the Easter story in with concern for the environment. Perhaps this holy season could provide inspiration for re-examining attitudes about our natural resources and the preservation of our ecological system.

I thought she had a good premise, and because I care about the future of the world I agreed to take part. The interview went roughly like this.

Interviewer: What are your earliest memories of any form of conservation?

Roy: I was born into a farm family. Farmers practised conservation to survive. For example, our woodlot was the only source of lumber, fuel for the home and sap for maple syrup. I was taught how to tap trees for sap in a non-damaging way. Old wood was cleared out to make room for young growth and new trees were planted when one was cut down. Crop rotation was practised instead of using herbicides, and fence rows were allowed to stand to prevent erosion and to give shelter to birds and small animals.

Interviewer: When did your fears for the environment begin?

Roy: When I was in my twenties I worked at a radio station in the Niagara district and saw the precious orchard land being dug up for subdivisions and paved over for parking lots. There are only two areas of this country where tender fruits such as peaches, grapes, nectarines and apricots can grow, and both the Niagara Peninsula and the Okanagan Valley are being destroyed.

Interviewer: Are you involved in helping conserve areas of this country?

Roy: Yes, two in particular. The Temagami region in Northern Ontario is unique in the world for its 400-year-old red and white pine, its 3,000-year-old aboriginal trails, and for being the world's source of the nearly extinct aurora trout. The Stein River Valley, British Columbia's largest chunk of untouched wilderness, is more than 44,000 acres of thick evergreens in the south-west part of that province and has become an environmental war zone. The Lytton and Mount Currie Indian bands call the land their "spiritual food." Mismanagement by both government and industry must be stopped before both areas are lost.

Interviewer: Why should we bring these concerns to people at this time of year?

Roy: Because Easter means renewal and beginning again. It also means confession for past sins and redemption to allow a new start. I'm not a theologian but it seems to me the idea of a new life for our endangered land, or a cleaning up of the atmosphere, is a very religious thing to consider.

Interviewer: The Book of Genesis says humankind was given dominion over the world and everything in it by God. Was Genesis wrong?

Roy: The interpretation is wrong. It says that God looked at the world and "it was good." All living things were in balance with one another. We were given the chance to be stewards of this creation.

Interviewer: We are told that the cost of reversing

present environment conditions would be $150 billion a
year. Can we afford it?

Roy: Considering that is only one sixth of the annual
$900 billion spend on armaments, it's a case of setting our
priorities.

Interviewer: Any other thoughts about Easter in this
regard?

Roy: Just that the night before he was crucified, Jesus
chose to spend time in a garden to pray and meditate. It
might be a good idea at Easter to pledge ourselves to create
and maintain more quiet garden spots before it's too late.

No Such Thing as a Healthy Tan
(UNPUBLISHED)

I recently stayed in one of those hotels where they slip a
morning newspaper under your door so you can read about
the state of the world before venturing into it. This particular paper's headline almost sent me back to bed. I've
seen a lot of headlines in my time, I've written quite a number of them and have even been in a few, but this was by
far the most shocking.

"Don't Let Your Children Play in the Sun," it read.

This was not on the lifestyle page, or in the science
section, but in big, bold letters across the top of the front
page. Canadians were being warned to stay out of the sun
and particularly not to expose their children to its rays.

What a tragedy! What a terrible thing we have done to our children! From the beginning of time, children have played in the sun. It is their birthright. We have managed to snatch it away from them by our greed, our selfishness and our carelessness.

In 1989, 517 people in Canada died of melanoma, the worst form of skin cancer, and more than 2,000 cases were diagnosed. The incidence of the disease has increased by more than 6 per cent in men since 1970. That was before scientists began to document the deterioration of the ozone layer, which filters out the sun's harmful ultraviolet rays. Now, 300,000 new cases are expected world-wide by the end of the decade largely because of ozone-destroying chlorofluorocarbons.

Nations have taken some steps to curb the output of CFCs, but the ozone layer is deteriorating more rapidly than expected. Scientists are predicting a further 15 per cent thinning of the ozone layer over Canada this spring. The onus is on governments and industrialists to clean up their act but the final responsibility will rest with us. Will we pressure government and industry to reverse the problem? Or will we just lather on more sunblock and hope for the best?

Ottawa's immediate response to the terrible headline was to offer daily bulletins as to probable exposure risks. Later it announced the bulletins would be weekly, then more recently complained it was having trouble compiling the information on a regional basis. This conjures up a picture of Canadian families huddling around the radio each morning to find out whether or not it's safe to go outside. This is merely coping with a bad situation; it's not doing anything about it.

We mustn't let our friendly, life-giving sun become a deadly enemy. In his book *Earth in the Balance*, Vice-President Al Gore writes with powerful conviction and sincerity. He says, "We are creating a world that is hostile to wilderness, that seems to prefer concrete to natural landscape. We have lost a sense of wonder and awe once inspired by a feeling of belonging and kinship with the rest of the living world." I think he has reminded us of a very important fact — air, water and sun are part of our very being. They are our life. When we destroy them, we destroy ourselves.

Perhaps now that we Canadians are under threat we can understand better the plight of others who share this planet with us. We live in a world where 1.7 billion people lack access to clean water. Where 25,000 people die from water-borne diseases every day. Where chemical production doubles in volume every seven to eight years. Where pesticides are made today at a rate 13,000 times faster than in 1962. Where the average North American citizen produces more than his or her weight in waste every day.

Are there solutions? There are certainly some strategic goals. We must stabilize world population. We must develop appropriate technologies. We must formulate ecological economies. And we must raise people's awareness around the world.

Do these goals sound impossible? I don't think so. But they must become priorities now if we want to see our children playing in the sun again.

The key to making these changes may lie in developing a positive attitude about the process.

Making the Most of Goodness and Joy
FEBRUARY 1990

I was chatting with a junior public service employee in Ottawa recently. He told me about picking up his boss, a deputy minister, at the airport on the latter's return from an overseas trip. In answer to the question "What's new?" the aide said, "Well, our department made the front page of the *Globe and Mail* this morning and we're being featured on *The Journal* tonight."

"Oh my God," said the senior official. "Where did we goof up?"

As a matter of fact, the news coverage was related to a research breakthrough his staff had made and was very complimentary.

The idea that media only report bad news is widespread.

It used to be that getting your name in the paper was a notable event. Now it brings fear and trepidation, and a common, ordinary phrase like "the press" often has a negative connotation.

Other words and phrases have suffered the same fate. Take the word *traffic*, which simply means the movement of vehicles or people from one place to another. Now it has a bad connotation and is associated with other negative words like *accident*, *tie-up* and *snarl*. On a flight out of Toronto recently, the pilot informed all the passengers, "There is no weather between here and Vancouver." Of course he meant no *bad* weather, but the word has come to mean trouble, delay and turbulence.

I think we should adopt a more positive perspective. Politicians for the most part are honest, hard-working people often doing a thankless job at great sacrifice. Most journalists I know are talented, dedicated individuals trying their best to be balanced and correct. Traffic does not necessarily mean a fender bender and weather can be wonderful.

For some time now, *feminist* has in many people's minds described a woman who is anti-men. A feminist is someone who advocates social and economic equality for women. Feminists can be either gender and it is not a pejorative word.

Look at the word *human*. Often when a person makes a mistake you hear, "Oh well, I'm only human," as though that was a lesser state of being. I would have thought that to be truly human would be one of the finest attainments in life.

With all the problems we face, I suppose we can understand why there are so many negative feelings around. Being aware of our hurting world through newspaper and magazine articles, seeing suffering faces on TV, does not foster a positive view of life. But any other approach would be self-defeating.

If we become bogged down in melancholy we will be of little use in seeking solutions. We can't change things for the better if we are constantly in a state of depression. I don't think it is a Pollyanna approach to look on the bright side. We want to protect our ecosystem because we enjoy the taste of fresh, clean water and the beauty of an unsullied sunset. We want to stamp out child abuse and neglect because we know the joys of holding children in our arms and watching them develop in a loving atmosphere. We want to end war because we've known peace.

In a television interview with Archbishop Anthony Bloom, head of the Russian Orthodox Church in England, we talked about the difficulty of finding joy in a world with so much sorrow. He told me, "Joy is an inward state. Pleasure and happiness are things that happen, but joy belongs to you. When things become too much I have learned not to rehearse yesterday's suffering and not to anticipate tomorrow's. I try and live within the day, and if that is too difficult, I divide the day into portions that can not only be endured but celebrated, drawing on the well of joy that I have known."

I'm not in favour of just putting on a "happy face." But I would like to see us adopt an attitude of appreciation for all the good things in our lives and work to preserve and foster them for the benefit of all.

There are some things, however, that no amount of polish can help.

Teaching City Folks to Respect Rural Ways
MAY 1990

When I was a boy growing up on an Ontario farm, I never received long lectures from my parents about honesty. The teacher in our one-room school did not hold classes in values education or invite special speakers to scare us into proper behaviour. We were expected to do the right thing and those who cared for us were very disappointed when we didn't. Somewhere along the line, things changed.

I still live on a farm but increasingly this pastoral paradise is being invaded by urbanites with a strangely distorted ethic.

Of course, some things never change. For years farmers have been waking up to see their ditches lined with debris tossed from the car trunks of city dwellers whose idea of recycling is to "dump it in the country." Rusty bed springs, mattresses, bottles and broken lawn ornaments festoon our side roads in competition with the emerging wildflowers.

Spring is the time of year when those puppies and kittens that looked so cute under the Christmas tree have become older, bothersome and pregnant. The next stop is a farmer's lawn or barnyard.

While these acts are inconsiderate and cruel, it's thievery that we find most difficult to understand. In the fall, where I live, apples and sweet corn are the main targets. Very often it's a family outing and the children are sent scampering into the fields to bring back bags of produce while the parents wait in the car.

Since I don't grow a lot of fruit or vegetables I was surprised on a visit to my "back 40" last week to see a car parked along the road and a family group at the edge of my woods digging out saplings and young evergreen shrubs.

"What's going on?" I asked.

"Oh, hi! We've just moved into a new subdivision where there are no trees or bushes so we're going to take these back and plant them in our yard."

"But they're mine."

"Well, you've got lots of them, for heaven's sake, you won't miss these."

"That's not the point. This is my property."

"I don't see any sign."

"I shouldn't have to put up a sign saying Don't Steal My Trees."

The mother and father looked at me as if I were the biggest grouch in the country. The children hung their heads.

In the end, I let them keep their booty but suggested perhaps next time they should stop at the farmhouse and ask permission since most farmers are happy to share, within reason. I also took the opportunity to deliver a short sermon to the parents about "setting an example."

The loss of a few shrubs is no big deal for me but the loss of a regular farmer's crop — a bushel here, a bushel there — can add up to a significant drain on an income that already shows the slimmest profit margin in our society.

Last autumn, I noticed a family in a station wagon drive past my house and slowly turn down the side road, hidden by the high corn in my neighbour's fields. The evening breeze brought back the sounds of excited voices and I could see the tops of the corn stalks breaking as ears were being ripped off. A short time later there was a slamming of doors and a spewing of gravel as the car sped off.

Why didn't I yell at them to get out? Why didn't I call the police or at least my neighbour to report these metropolitan miscreants?

Because I knew they were stealing Bishop 30-28, known by farmers in my area of Canada as the hardiest hybrid variety of silage corn. Sometimes called hard corn or cow corn, these lovely fat cobs look scrumptious, but no amount of boiling will change them from tasteless, tooth-cracking bullets of fodder.

Bon appétit. Score one for our side.

Recycling Old Values for a Better Tomorrow
AUGUST 1990

Long before *biodegradable* and *recycling* became such common words in our modern language, both were happening as a matter of course in our daily living habits. Those of us who lived in a less affluent time saw less waste. When the axiom "A penny saved is a penny earned" was a part of our childhood understanding of life, nothing was discarded.

Milk, for example, came straight from the cow to the table if you lived in rural areas. In the city, it came to your doorstep in reusable glass bottles. Plastic hadn't been invented yet. The backyard garden provided fresh fruit and vegetables in season and our winter supplies were canned in mason jars that had been handed down for generations.

Our cellar was a supermarket of food and delicacies just a few feet away from the kitchen. Long shelves bent under the weight of hundreds of jars filled with preserved beans, corn, stewed tomatoes, relish, peaches, plums, pears, jams and several kinds of pickles. There were crocks of homemade butter, and cheese that aged and grew more interesting over the winter months.

This was why at an early age all of us kids were taught to whistle. One of our chores was to "go fetch" from the cellar when it was meal preparation time. The instructions went something like this: "I need a dish of butter, a jar of ginger tomatoes and a basket of potatoes, so pucker up." Our parents knew that as long as they could hear us whistle we weren't sampling a jar of peaches, stealing a slab of cheese or, depending on our age, siphoning a fast sip from the cider barrel.

Table scraps were fed to the house pets. If they desired more exotic fare there were always plenty of mice around. Very few cans of any kind ever entered the house. The ones that did were cleaned and used to store things like nails, bolts, pins or buttons. Clothes were passed down from parents to children and from one sibling to the next. Holes and rips were patched and mended. Has anyone darned a sock in the last 25 years? Apparel of all kinds eventually ended up in a "rag bag," where much of it was sewn into homemade quilts called crazy quilts. It was comforting, just before dozing off at night, to look at your coverlet and see recognizable scraps of material from your family's favourite clothing.

Newspapers, magazines and catalogues had two very important functions. One was to start the morning fires in the wood stoves and the other was to stock the outdoor privy. Only the highest-quality publications went there.

Potato peelings, lettuce leaves and other residue from meal preparation went on the garden compost heap.

I find it interesting how little we've learned over the years. On our farm we delivered our milk to the local cheese factory and we would refill our milk cans with the whey left over from the previous day's production. This, mixed with ground grain, formed the basis of our pigs' daily menu.

Two years ago, the U.S. Department of Agriculture, concerned about the large amount of whey dairies and cheese factories were dumping into streams, launched a $200,000 research project. Guess what? They found that it could be recycled as nutritious feed for farm animals.

No one really wants to go back to those wood-chopping, water-hauling days of yesteryear. Advances in science and technology have provided us with an abundant and enjoyable lifestyle. But we have also developed a throwaway mentality that has buried us in mountains of garbage and a sea of pollution. Perhaps what we should recycle are the old-fashioned ethics of thrift, prudence and common sense.

Foam Lake, Saskatchewan:
The Best Place in the World

MAY 1996

One place where many old-fashioned values survive is Foam Lake, Saskatchewan, officially designated "The Best Place to Live in the World."

The small town north-west of Yorkton has achieved the honour in a perfectly legitimate and painstaking manner. Last year the United Nations put out a Human Development Report, as it does every year. For the past six years part of the report has been a Human Development Index made up of three components that would indicate the best conditions under which to live. Taken into consideration are life expectancy at birth, education and adjusted measure of income per capita. For the past three years, according to the United Nations, Canada has come out on top as the best place in the world to live.

This year, a Canadian research group called Infometrica took the study a bit further. Adding some criteria specific to Canada, Infometrica established the best province in the best country in the world. For the most part, adjusted income and education matched across Canada. Saskatchewan won on life expectancy. In that province the average life expectancy is 78.29 years, the highest in Canada.

Enter CBC Radio's *Morning Edition*, Saskatchewan's early-morning news, weather and information show, hosted by Sheila Coles. She and her producers decided to invite listeners to pick the best town in the best province in the best country in the world. Foam Lake took the top spot. I think what tipped the scales was a wonderfully descriptive letter sent to the program by relative newcomer Joan Eyolfson Cadham, who told of the warmth and love of the residents of Foam Lake and district as they welcomed her husband and her to the community, then held and supported her as they mourned together her husband's untimely death.

I had to go to Foam Lake and take a look for myself. I just couldn't resist paying a visit to the best place in the world. It's a neat, pretty town at the edge of the prairie where rolling hills begin. The namesake lake bubbled and foamed at one time because of limestone deposits around its edge. Now the lake is reedy and unusable except for ducks. There are some fine stores and a lovely community centre, but it is not the facilities or the scenery that sets this place apart. It is the people. They actually work together for the good of the community. The commercial sector, the school boards, the social services, the elected officials, the local newspaper — all act in concert to deal with both problems and opportunities. What an interesting concept!

I can take you to many other towns and cities across this country where conflict in municipal matters is the order of the day. I have attended council meetings where members constantly squabble each other into a state of inactivity. Town improvement projects are stalled by bickering merchants. Environmental initiatives fail for lack of agreement on procedure. School boards stagnate. The religious community dons its blinkers. Those who try to organize a sense of town spirit and cooperation finally give up and move away in despair.

Foam Lake reminds me of another small town I visited many years ago. It was St. Paul, Alberta, a town of a little over 5,000 people north-east of Edmonton. It had, through a series of fundraising events, collected close to $1 million for charity. They got in touch with Mother Teresa of Calcutta and said if she wanted the money to come and get it. She came. This was the same town that built a landing pad for alien spaceships in 1967 in case they wanted to come and wish Canadians a happy birthday during our Centennial year.

Maybe having a healthy sense of humour is part of the equation for successful communities. In St. Paul and Foam Lake, we talked about many serious subjects in meetings with the citizens and yet I felt that sense of joy and fun people get when they join hands in common causes. Is Foam Lake, Saskatchewan, the best place in the world to live? As far as I'm concerned, you bet!

Indeed, the best part about travelling is meeting people and the fresh perspective it gives you on things on the home front.

A Refreshing Change From Constant Griping

OCTOBER 1991

Earlier in the year, as a result of writing a book, I was sent on an author's tour. This is a gruelling regimen imposed by publishers ostensibly to encourage sales, but I think it is secretly to ensure that you won't write another book. For a couple of weeks, your whole world becomes a blur of newspaper interviews, open-line radio programs, late-night talk shows, bookstore signings and luncheon speeches. You see the cities and towns of Canada only through the windows of airplanes, hotels, restaurants and broadcasting studios. But you do talk to a lot of people. They tell you their joys and frustrations, their hopes for themselves, their families and their country. It's saddening to hear the complaints about high taxes, unemployment, curtailed services and lack of housing. There is a despondency rampant in the land that seems contagious, spreading to all walks of life, age groups and geographical locations. Some blame the government, some the media, some big business or American domination.

Thankfully, another spirit is alive and well. I sensed hope and determination when callers told me about their involvement in social action groups, human rights organizations or environmental causes. Teachers seemed proud and encouraged by many of the young people in their classrooms and parents talked of closer communication with their children. Perhaps tough times bring out the best in some people. I think that most still agree Canada is a great place to live.

My other travels this year took me to Scandinavia. A tour down the northern coast of Norway, a visit to southern Sweden and several days in Copenhagen, Denmark — different countries, different people, but with many of the same concerns. The major difference I found was one of attitude.

In Denmark, for example, the Value Added Tax is 22 per cent, compared with our 7 per cent GST. Personal income and business taxes are also high. There is no tipping because 15 per cent is automatically added to your restaurant bill or taxi charge. It is a very expensive place to live, yet I did not hear one complaint. As a matter of fact, it was with great pride that they talked of their free education from pre-school through university, their complete health care from cradle to grave, their guaranteed housing for senior citizens and their $12 dollar an hour minimum wage.

If bilingualism bothers you, Norway is not the place for you. Historically, Norway relied entirely on oral tradition. No written form of Norwegian existed until the fourteenth century, when the invading Danes decided it was necessary. Old Norwegian therefore closely resembles Danish. All citizens must learn Old Norwegian. Then an independently minded scholar developed New Norwegian, which gave written symbols to the old Norse tongue. All citizens must learn this form of Norwegian as well. They must also respond to any letters written to them in precisely the form it was received. The aboriginal people of Finmark (northern Norway), the Lapps or Sami, also speak their native tongue, which is vaguely reminiscent of Hungarian. All Norwegians start to learn English at the age of eight or nine and must continue to study it throughout their education.

How do you feel about the monarchy? Danes love Queen Margrethe II and her family. In a recent survey they overwhelmingly voted to continue her rule and 85 per cent said if they ever were to become a republic, they wanted her for president. They are also very fond of their prime minister, a Conservative, who rides to work each morning on a bicycle. They have the most stringent environmental regulations in the world, and the purity of their water and the cleanliness of their cities show it.

After all my travels, I'm glad to be home. My family has been in this wonderful country for seven generations and there is nowhere else on earth I'd sooner live. But now and then it's nice to be among people who aren't complaining and harping about their government or their lot in life, and who have built a prosperous and caring society that knows how to laugh and have fun.

Orchestrated Protest versus Honest Dissent

NOVEMBER 1991

One of the great things about living in a country like Canada is the freedom to dissent. We are actually urged to express our opposition to statements made or positions taken by any organization or individual.

Almost all newspapers and magazines have a "Letters to the Editor" column. Radio stations maintain open-line shows and answering machines that allow listeners to give their two cents' worth on any topic under the sun. Public opinion polls are followed closely by the business community and the political sector of our society.

I applaud the right to disagree. I am cheered that people take the time and trouble to write, phone or wave banners proclaiming their stand on any issue.

Where the process fails to impress me is at the point when the opposition becomes orchestrated into a carbon-copy expression of dissent.

An example. This past year I was involved in some television commercials for a Canadian trust company that tied its message in with a campaign to help promote environmental concern. Part of the commercial pitch offered a booklet that gave viewers various simple suggestions that could be followed to help protect the planet's ecosystem. In one section, the booklet claimed that the raising of meat took too great a toll on the earth's resources. It went on to criticize the use of antibodies, hormones and chemicals in our farming practices.

Several sections of the Canadian farming community took strong exception to these remarks and responded with a flood of letters to the trust company and to me. Fair enough. But what intrigued me was both the variety of concerned organizations and the unity of their responses. Not just the beef, pork and poultry farmers were up in arms, but also the bean and potato growers, veterinarians, home economists, biologists and agrologists.

Did all those people really see the commercials? Of course not. They were advised of the dastardly deed we committed and were urged to respond *en masse*. After reading the first dozen or so letters, you could see how carefully orchestrated the write-in campaign had been managed. The first paragraphs were original, but the remaining pages of each letter were identical. Obviously they had been copied from a circulated form letter with instructions as to how to address the envelope.

After a while a campaign like this loses its effect. A few original letters of complaint would have made the point and attracted more attention.

This overkill method of protest is familiar to anyone in the communications business. For years the Catholic Women's League used to mail out pre-printed postcards that went something like this: "We the undersigned deplore most strongly your reference to (subject) which was heard on your station on (day) at (time). Please be advised that we will not only encourage a boycott of your station among other listeners but with your advertisers as well if any reference to (subject) is made by your station in the future."

These would promptly arrive by the bushel after some program dealing even remotely with such subjects as abortion, contraception or criticism of the separate school system had aired.

In the early '70s I went to Belfast to interview Protestant and Catholic factions for a television documentary on Northern Ireland's religious violence. About a month after returning to Canada, the CBC started receiving a slew of letters saying the program on Northern Ireland broadcast in the *Man Alive* series had been one-sided, distorted, libellous, unfair and a downright disgrace. The fact was the program was still in the editing and packaging stage. It hadn't gone on the air yet.

I'm sure members of Parliament and government committees must feel the same frustration when they receive tons of mail from some printing or copying machine, identical right down to the exclamation marks.

How much more effective a simple, clearly written, original note would be to put forward a person's concern. It would certainly have a much better chance of being read and acted upon.

Beavers Be Dammed!

APRIL 1997

Canadians are famous for their ability to mount protests of all kinds, but especially in the field of animal rights.

We have come a long way in our treatment of animals in this country even in my lifetime. As a young farm boy I can remember our family shooting groundhogs and squirrels, trapping rabbits and mice, killing crows and starlings. At our rural public school boys were paid five cents for a groundhog tail and two cents for a starling beak. We never thought twice about chopping up a snake that was discovered in the garden or while digging a fence post hole. Even our domestic cat or dog generally foraged for its own food and usually slept outside.

My children were born in the city, but when we moved to a farm in the '70s they of course wanted horses. After walking over the fields and seeing all the places where groundhogs had burrowed, I explained we would have to kill these pests because the holes could easily mean broken legs for our larger animals. This suggestion was met with protests of horror and an ingenious solution. The next day they had shoved long poles in the holes that would warn the horses but allow the groundhogs to come and go.

I learned a lot from my children. Now if someone accidentally catches a fish as they troll a lazy summer line, it gets tossed back. Animals and birds are shot with cameras and the results lovingly mounted in albums. We all have been in homes where the fireplace has a bearskin rug in front and a set of antlers above but we leave as soon as we can. We do not join our neighbours in the annual deer-hunting season and refuse to allow hunters on our land. We feed the birds and squirrels all winter long, mice and frogs are rescued from the backyard pool and, while I am still not fond of snakes, I now would never kill one.

This kind of attitude is fine for a person like me who does not depend on the killing of animals for income or for survival. Because of where I live, I don't have a problem with predators. I also have no crops at risk from animals scavenging for food. This is not the case for all Canadians, so I find myself in great sympathy with people who defend their right to hunt and kill. I have visited many northern communities where the frozen carcass of a seal or caribou next to the house is a guarantee of making it through until spring. Many of my neighbours grow corn both for seed and the canning factory and, while they try their best to ward off the marauding raccoons with loud "bangers" that explode at intervals during the night, the only sure prevention of crop ruination is the shotgun.

Arguments for and against the killing of some animals fall into a grey area without easy or comfortable answers.

Even someone whom most of us consider the foremost animal lover of all time had a dark side. I have always been a supporter of the Audubon Society and an admirer of John J. Audubon, its founder. His very name has come to signify love of nature and environmental protection. I was surprised to hear what a predator he was. To get that distinctive natural look that became his trade mark he would wire freshly killed specimens onto a board with a grid design and then paint them. "I shot the first kingfisher I met, pierced the body with wire, fixed it to the board with another wire holding its head and one for its feet. This was my first of many drawings actually from nature," he recounted in a *New York Times* interview.

Before the turn of the century there were Audubon Gun Clubs. It is suggested that far more birds fell to Audobon's gun than were needed for drawing or research. Most of the ornithologists who followed him were apparently equally fond of the gun. How do we feel about killing for art's sake?

The question I have to face is, How do I feel about killing for my property's sake? For a number of years we have had families of beavers on our farm. We have watched them with delight as they gnawed down trees in the swamp, built their dams, reared their pups and frolicked in the dammed creek. It's not funny any more. The dam has become so big it has wiped out several acres of adjoining fields. The water has risen so high several hives of bees are in danger of being inundated. Do I shoot them? Do I trap them? If I destroy the dam I can violate environmental legislation. If my removal of the dam causes them to starve or freeze I am committing an offence under the Canadian Criminal Code.

See my problem? I'm damned if I do and dammed if I don't.

The other area of protest that has always seen Canadian involvement has been opposition to nuclear proliferation.

Banning the Bombs
FEBRUARY 1997

After more than 100 million people signed a petition early last year asking for the elimination of nuclear weapons, the United Nations World Court responded by suggesting their use could very well be illegal. In the closing months of the year, 60 military officers from the United States, Russia, Britain, France and 12 other countries joined to urge disarmament. It has taken us a long time finally to see the light.

The horror of Hiroshima stunned many around the world, but not enough to influence governments' decisions to build bigger and better nuclear weapons. When it was announced in 1949 that the Soviet Union had exploded a nuclear device, most Canadians were thankful that American technology was working at full speed to keep ahead of the arms race. In the meantime we would have to learn how to protect ourselves.

When I think back to those days, I marvel at our naïveté. Did we really think that hiding under desks at school would save us from a nuclear blast? And what about all those civil defence organizations that showed us what route to take out of town when the bomb hit? Backyard shelters built of concrete blocks and stocked with dried food were a popular safeguard against atomic annihilation, and just knowing where to turn our radio dial in the event of an attack seemed to give us a sense of security.

I remember doing on-the-spot coverage of a simulated nuclear bomb attack on Niagara Falls, arranged jointly by the Canadian and American civil defence organizations. They were pretending that the Russians had bombed the Niagara hydroelectric station and people in a 50-mile radius were to be evacuated. Citizens from both sides of the border volunteered to be victims and were made up with fake cuts, burns and ketchup-soaked clothing, then propped up against trees and doorways. A building was set on fire and several teams of firefighters from the area rushed in and quickly doused it with water. Ambulances were called and passing motorists were stopped to take survivors to local hospitals whose staffs continued the farce by applying dressings and splints to the ersatz wounds.

It was all done in deadly earnest and made an exciting broadcast, but I have often wondered if we really thought we were learning how to survive or if we were fooling ourselves even then.

I was thinking about this recently as I was reading the autobiography of Dr. Helen Caldicott, who in my mind did more than anyone to turn the nations of the world against nuclear armaments. While today she tends to hurl her considerable wrath against polluters and multinationals, she will always be remembered for her graphic and electrifying anti-nuclear speeches that stirred millions in the '70s.

I recall one interview I did with her when she was living in New York after she had founded Physicians for Social Responsibility. I mentioned to her that most Canadians felt helpless since it was the superpowers that called the shots in regard to the nuclear race.

"Well, you Canadians are going to be killed too, aren't you?" she asked. "So will the Mexicans, because you're all part of the North American continent. If I was a Canadian, I'd be hopping mad because they're fooling around with your lives. And how dare the superpowers behave like nine-year-old boys saying 'I've got more bombs than you've got'? That's totally inappropriate in the nuclear age. Ninety-two per cent of the world's people don't live in the superpowers and they should rise up and stop these two crazy giants behaving the way they do."

Well, we did rise up. Because of people like Dr. Caldicott we have managed to reduce the nuclear arsenal. We still have a distance to go, however, before we can be completely free of the nuclear threat. Caldicott herself says we all have to get back into the fight to prevent smaller nations from arming. Current arms control pacts leave the U.S. and Russia with 3,500 warheads each by 2003. That gives the smaller nuclear powers little incentive to reduce their stockpiles.

4

FAMILY
RECIPES

*"The little world of childhood with its familiar
surroundings is a model of the greater world.
The more intensively the family has stamped
its character upon the child, the more it will
tend to feel and see its earlier miniature world
again in the bigger world of adult life."*

— CARL JUNG, *PSYCHOLOGICAL REFLECTIONS:
A JUNG ANTHOLOGY*

Male by Birth, Feminist by Choice
JUNE 1992

I feel very fortunate that, throughout my life, I have had
close associations with interesting women. When I hear

of today's "Iron Johns" who are trying to resurrect their lost maleness or middle-age-crisis sufferers complaining about the rise of feminism, I thank the women of my past and present just for being around.

I grew up in a home where there was no such thing as men's work and women's work. There was just work. My mother and sisters laboured side by side with my father and brothers in the fields. They drove the horses, pitched hay and slopped the hogs as well and likely better than the rest of us. Sweeping the house, washing dishes or clothes, even darning our socks was not foreign to the men. I could even knit one and purl two when I was ten.

When I began a radio career I worked for Mary Burgoyne. In those days she was the only female manager of a radio station in Canada. There are a few more today, but not many. She was one of the most decisive, strong-willed, yet caring and compassionate persons I had ever met. She taught me a lot about broadcasting, but more importantly taught, by example, the responsibility those of influence have to the community. She programmed her station with the listener in mind. Even when some productions were not commercially viable, she insisted they be aired.

During those younger years, I was certainly aware of the inequality our society accorded women. In journalism and broadcasting, my chosen professions, women wrote for the "ladies' page" or produced the "social notes programs." They almost never wrote news, or sports or editorials. Yet I kept running into women who were exceptions to the rule.

When the Anglican, Roman Catholic and United Churches joined their communications departments to present a unified voice to the industry, women were in the forefront. People like Nancy Edwards, Dickie Sada, Dorothy Forbes, Alice Christian, Bonnie Brennan, Alice Foster, Heather Dau and others were pioneers for those who came after and respected colleagues for those of us fortunate enough to work with them.

My years with CBC-Television involved working with women at every level. Here, again, it was not as easy for women to climb the professional ladder as it was for men. Only in recent years have women in media made the kinds of inroads they deserve. But my department saw an abundance of women producers with, in charge of us all as executive producer, Louise Lore, one of Canada's most creative and dedicated broadcasters.

My life today is made richer by the women who are near. My wife, Jane, and daughters, Mandy and Lesley, are strong individuals who know who they are, are pleased with themselves and contribute in very special ways to those around them. I would describe all three as feminists in the true sense of that word — but then, so am I.

To me, being a feminist is not, as some believe, going around knocking men but trying to see the world through the eyes of women, then acting accordingly. How does it feel to be denied roles in society because of your sex? How do you handle a situation when you are patronized and looked upon as the "weaker sex"? Where do you get the strength to carry on when as a single mother you are denied proper work benefits or daycare facilities?

The struggle for sexual equality is certainly not over. Women are still very much at the bottom of our social system. A well-known Canadian community worker was quoted recently as saying, "Most women are still one man away from poverty."

I'm quite happy being a man, but I know how much I owe to women and I would like to do what I can to balance the scales of justice. After all, I've got five granddaughters coming along who are expecting the world to be a fair place.

Another thing I've learned from women is that satisfaction that can come from a creative, conversation-filled kitchen.

The Joys of Making and Breaking Bread
SEPTEMBER 1992

My mother taught her large brood to cook, bake and fry as soon as we were tall enough to reach the top of the stove. Not only would this knowledge be of assistance to her but she knew that someday we would be on our own and, at least then, be able to feed ourselves. Nothing fancy was imparted in these lessons, just basic techniques as to temperatures, proportions, timing and her own personal tricks such as how to prepare gravy without lumps. Now, in a time when a can-opener or a microwave is all that's really required, I find more satisfaction than ever in "doing it from scratch."

According to a Canadian Press report, I must be in the minority. It found that more and more people today are choosing not to cook their own meals or don't know how. Cold cereal is apparently becoming the supper of the culinarily challenged. Convenience foods like popcorn, toast, canned soup and beans are joining take-out favourites such as pizza, burgers and Chinese food as the dinners of choice. A glass of instant breakfast drink mix is being touted as a popular replacement for real food.

Ken Bouchard, who teaches cooking to singles through the continuing education program at the Ottawa Board of Education, blames television. He says, "The current generation aged 20 to 40 just did not have to do as much in the kitchen as the generation before them. They had television or they were busy with after-school activities. I'm amazed at how many people do not know the very basic techniques of cooking."

I suppose that if people want to eat prepared, plastic-tasting food, that's their business. What I regret is that they may never know the special joy that is inherent in the preparation and serving of one's own creative efforts.

My specialty is bread — all kinds of bread. From pungent, chewy sourdough to delicate flaky, *croissants au beurre*. For me, the variety of textures, the kneading to combine the ingredients, the risings, to say nothing of the aroma that fills the house, is magical. It has been a long time since our family has depended on store-bought bread.

There is something almost mystical in mixing and shaping loaves of dough. You realize you are part of a process that began 6,000 years before the birth of Christ. Over the years bread has been honoured and made sacred. In her book *The Rituals of Dinner*, Margaret Visser points out, "We still remember that breaking of bread, and sharing it with friends, means friendship itself, and also trust, pleasure and gratitude in the sharing. The Latin word 'companion' means literally 'a person with whom we share bread.'"

I look after most of the baking at our house. Even though I'm not fond of desserts I love making cakes, pies and muffins for visitors. My wife, Jane, is better at pasta dishes, meats and casseroles than I, so in concert meal preparation is a delightful adventure and, according to our guests, well worth the effort.

Very often our guests are grandchildren who enter wholeheartedly into the cooking game. Most children I know like mucking around in flour and water. When they take ordinary paste, add yeast, sugar and butter and watch it turn into something they can spread with jam, it becomes an experience they never forget. I recommend bagels as a start in cooking for kids. Twisting the dough into circles, watching them bob in boiling water and then turn puffy and golden brown in the oven beats any hour of television cartoons or video game.

There are many ways to look at it. Home cooking is certainly cheaper. (I figure my bread, for example, runs about 13 cents per loaf.) It inevitably tastes better. (Chemicals and preservatives aren't necessary.) It's an activity that the family can enjoy together. (It's hard to share the excitement of a Kraft dinner.)

But, most importantly, in an increasingly technological and computerized society, cooking gives us a chance to express ourselves creatively and share our handiwork with others.

Whrrr, Bzzz, Zap — Pop Goes the Family
NOVEMBER 1990

Is it my imagination, or are modern kitchens getting smaller? It seems like the large old country kitchen, with its huge table able to accommodate a family of a dozen or so, is already a thing of the past.

That's possibly because modern circumstances no longer throw the family together. The structures of Canadian life are centrifugal, driving families apart. The fast pace of our lives, the many outside attractions and the economic realities of making a living result in a family where members seldom meet, or if they do, the encounter is brief and harried.

Often father, mother and children operate on different agendas. Throughout the day we spend our time with fellow workers or classmates, then at night we turn on our TVs to watch other people's lives or put on our earphones to listen to other people's music.

I don't expect everyone to gather around the parlour piano any more or play Parcheesi by the fireplace, but I do resent what is happening in the family kitchen. Traditionally, here is where the family came together. Not only was it an interesting place to be but there were chores to do and you could help each other out. With today's modern appliances one lone person can handle kitchen duties.

"You peel and I'll chop." Remember that phrase? This always gave us plenty of time to ask the question "How was your day?" If it was a good day we shared the joy. If it was a bad day we gave comfort. Now, you dump everything into the food processor and *whrrr*, the job is done.

"You keep an eye on the meat loaf and I'll start the gravy." This was a great time to discuss an article you had read or to help with a tough homework problem. No more. Now you take a frozen package out of the freezer, pop it into the microwave, press a button and *zap*, supper's ready.

"You wash and I'll dry." This was a working-together

time where you shared that funny story you were told or heard about the home run that almost was. Forget it. Now everything goes into the electric dishwasher where, after a short *bzzz*, the dishes stay sparkling clean until the next meal.

I've never owned a microwave and I doubt if I ever will, despite its apparent advantage to a busy family. I like the smell of food cooking. The aroma of a busy kitchen is part of the pleasure of dining. I also like the sound of bacon sizzling and soup bubbling. Automatic coffee-makers have taken away that delicious sound of coffee perking.

I realize that with modern appliances we are supposed to be saving valuable time, but in the long run we may be losing it. It seems to me that when we replace sizzling, bubbling and percolating with *whrrr*, *bzzz* and *zap*, we miss something. Most of all, we miss the family helping out in the kitchen.

'Til Death Do Us Part ... Or Maybe Not
JULY 1990

Maybe it's the lack of homey contact that's contributing to our apparently ever-increasing divorce rate. I am having trouble trying to remember which of my friends are still married, recently divorced, just separated or only living together. It's especially difficult with invitations to parties, or bringing your address book up to date. How do you address an envelope to Howard Jones and his "main squeeze"?

Marriages are falling apart at an unprecedented rate these days. Sociologists tell us that divorces are happening to one out of every three couples. But statistics also show that weddings are becoming more popular. An increasing number are choosing to tie the marital knot instead of living common law.

Lawyers are telling us what a good idea it is to sign a marriage contract. Before taking the big step the happy couple is advised to decide how their worldly goods will be divided if the split comes. This may be a very sensible approach to the economics of life, but it seems as though we are entering into marriage with divorce on our minds.

Whatever happened to pledges and vows and promises? They don't seem to be mentioned in a lot of modern wedding ceremonies. I was at one such wedding a couple of months ago where the bride and groom wrote their own order of service. They used favourite poetry and quotes from literature instead of the formal rites I remember. They borrowed liberally from the Lebanese poet and mystic Kahlil Gibran, who was a literary find of the '20s and a rediscovery of the love-in crowd of the '60s. Gibran wrote such lines as "Let there be spaces in your togetherness." This is likely very good advice, but at the point in the service where the highest moment of commitment usually comes, this couple put in more qualifications and codicils than a Philadelphia lawyer back in the days when marriages were arranged by mutually suspicious families.

"I will love you," they said to each other, "as long as things are meaningful between us." I gather this is intended to be a sign of high regard for the protection of personal integrity, but for me it left something out. What it does not suggest is that somewhere down the road these two may be required to lean on each other. There is no indication that loneliness might occur or that rough times may call for a "cleaving to one another."

Today's society puts unprecedented strains on marriage. Separate careers are often necessary to pay the rent and buy the groceries. Our fast-paced technological world is not conducive to long, intimate reflections on those promises we made when our whole happy lives stretched out before us. Unless our vows were meaningful and deep, sometimes all it takes is a small bump on the road of life to throw us off track. "Pledging one's troth" may sound silly but it sure beats a lot of "spaces in one's togetherness."

While "'til death do us part" may very well be an outmoded concept, I see nothing wrong with phrases such as "for richer for poorer" or "in sickness and in health." We're talking commitment here — a dedication to each other, a realization that no matter what happens we're both in this together, an understanding that not every day is "meaningful."

When a marriage disintegrates, of course there should be separation or divorce. It's sad, even damaging when a couple feels bound together because they feel it's "the thing to do," or "for the sake of the children." But I think more marriages would succeed if partners committed themselves to each other at the very beginning instead of preparing themselves for divorce during the wedding.

I know that not all marriages are made in heaven, but few can survive the hell of not trying.

Marriages do not need to be on the rocks for children to suffer. Sometimes couples who stay together create an atmosphere their offspring simply can't stand.

Losing Marcia
MARCH 1997

I saw her out of the corner of my eye standing aside, away from the crowd, watching me. It was a book-signing event at a shopping mall in Calgary, part of the inevitable tour that publishers arrange to introduce one's latest opus. When the last dedication had been inscribed and we were packing up the remaining editions she approached and asked if I had a few moments to talk. I did.

"My name is Marcia Hunt," she said. "I live in Alberta and I think we are related. When I was little and living at home, now and again we would see you on TV. My father always claimed that you were a relative. I don't know how we are supposed to be related and maybe he didn't know either because he never explained. My father ran away from home when he was 15 and would never talk about his parents. I guess he was sort of the black sheep in the family. I became the next generation's black sheep and left home when I was 16. I'm now 24. The point is, I have no idea about my family history. Can you help me?"

When she told me her father's name I said I remembered him as a little boy and that his father had been my cousin. I told her about her grandparents and how much I had liked them when I was young. I recalled stories of family get-togethers and explained who her ancestors had been, where they had come from, and some of their accomplishments. Then I stopped. She had started to cry. There on a cement bench near a gurgling water fountain in a secluded corner of a western mall, I held her while she quietly sobbed.

I guess until then I never realized the importance of our own personal history. I took it for granted that family memories were passed on. Certainly as a youngster I pestered my parents to tell me stories about their ancestors, as my children clamoured for information about theirs. The walls of our old farm home were hung with sombre pictures of long-dead relatives and I thrilled to hear their tales. Bequeathed furniture, dishes and knick-knacks scattered throughout the house kept them real and alive in my imagination. Some of these items still remain in my home today. My children have had them as part of their lives and I have told and retold the stories. But, what would it be like to look back and see a blank wall? What is it like to always wonder what parts of our personality were formed by others so long ago? I wouldn't care if I had discovered rascals and rogues among my kith and kin as long as I had the opportunity to put form to them through the remembrances of others.

But what if for some reason you don't grow up with family or neighbours who "knew you when"? What if parents split up and little is known of the other partner's heritage? What if you are an adopted child and all that's known of your family is printed on some official form? In an increasingly impersonal society I think it is important we all do what we can to help establish identity.

At the University of Regina, I was part of a Seniors Studies Program project that resulted in a book of memoirs by a number of older men and women who recounted stories of their past that not only made interesting reading for all of us but I'm sure were a delight to members of their families. Whether we feel we have the ability to write down our history or if we just verbally pass it on, I think it is very important for our younger family members in helping them understand who they are.

Recently we had a large family reunion. It was the first

one for many years. Relatives came from across the country to gather together for a long weekend of remembering old faces, being introduced to new ones, laughing at shared experiences and taking pleasure in nostalgic memories of those family members who are no longer with us. It occurred to me several times that weekend as I watched the horde of children gambolling, giggling and conversing with their elders that they were not only discovering family but in a real way discovering themselves.

I had tried to contact Marcia long before the event. My newsletter, which was mailed to every known relative, was also mailed to the address she had given me. It came back: "Not at this address."

I'm very sorry we've lost her again.

The Pitter-Patter of our Mortality
JULY 1992

I believe one of the greatest joys of family life is being a grandfather. It is an entirely unique paternal relationship. It is looser, more flexible than being a father. No matter how hard I tried with my own children, there was a tendency to hover. Because of fear or uncertainty or insecurity, I sometimes found myself interfering too often, thinking I knew best, not letting go.

Grandchildren are different. For the most part they are someone else's responsibility. Someone else clothes, feeds and shelters them. They are only visiting. When I become too bossy or cloying, they go home. We see each other at our very best. We love each other in a no-pressure, fun-time atmosphere.

I have seven grandchildren from five to ten years of age. Twice a year, the families all visit at once and the old farmhouse explodes with noise and energy. Most of the time, the grandchildren come in ones or twos and the stillness of the country is matched by our quiet times as we read, talk and dream together.

Back behind the garden is the "magic path." It was called this by the older grandchildren when they were two or three. It is where they always saw rabbits, chipmunks and birds' nests, heard bees, frogs and the wind, discovered moss, wildflowers, and strange footprints.

Near the end of the path is "little half-tree." We found this white pine when it was a tiny sapling about two feet in height with branches only on one side. The taller trees had blocked the light and it was struggling to survive. Over the years, it has reached for the sun and now towers over all of us. High up on its lopsided limbs can be seen several Christmas balls left by visiting grandchildren to let it share in our happy time.

A walk down the magic path is really an excuse to talk. This is where I hear about mean teachers, troublesome friends and the frustration of having parents. It gives me a chance to tell about special teachers I have met, friends I have kept all my life and how their moms or dads behaved when they were young. When all else fails, grandfathers can always revert to the old line, "You think you've got it bad? Why, when I was your age ..."

They are fascinated with the past. After they have been tucked in for the night and the last book has been read comes the inevitable request, "Tell me a story about when you were a little boy." They listen in amazement to tales of a life before Nintendo, compact discs or television. "What games did you play? What songs did you sing? What did you look at?" These moments are part of a ritual that has continued since families began, where, at the end of the day, the elders tell tales of an earlier time.

Sometimes you find yourself looking at them and wondering what the future holds in store. Sometimes your heart breaks for them. With your own children you can see what has happened — your hopes or fears for them have been realized. But what about their little ones? The world today seems to be a much scarier place. A simple walk to the store or a chat with a stranger is not recommended. The implications of a kiss or a hug must be considered. Far too often conversations become warnings about dangers we never heard of when we were their age. There is guilt in passing on to them a scarred and brutal world. But there is also pride in the fact that our generation has assured them of a healthier and longer life, more freedom from ignorance and a better sense of worth.

I think grandchildren also serve another very important role. They remind you of your own mortality. To acknowledge their youth is to realize your age. While to a daughter or son you can be a pal, a colleague or a fellow traveller, to a grandchild you are *always* old. These young people will be around long after you're gone. They will carry, for more years than anyone you know, the memory of this old presence in their lives. Through them you live the longest. Because of this, every grandchild is a bit of heaven.

5

PRACTICAL
POLITICS

*"Everything in our political life tends
to hide from us that there is anything
wiser than our ordinary selves."*

— MATTHEW ARNOLD, *BARBARIANS,
PHILISTINES, POPULACE*

Is There Intelligent Political Life Here?
AUGUST 1993

To paraphrase Solomon: Rise up, my beloved Canadian,
my registered voter, and make a choice. For lo, the term
of office is past, Mulroney is over and gone. The election
posters appear on the earth. The time of the pollster is
come and the voice of the politician is heard in the land.

And what a voice! We've been inundated with political rhetoric since the year began and we still have weeks to go before the cacophony fades. Provincial elections and a leadership race have added to the abundance of campaign verbiage, and it's hard not to feel a sense of confusion and perhaps helplessness as we slowly drown in a sea of promises, pledges and patronage.

Here are some questions I've been wondering about.

Who's minding the store? While our Cabinet ministers and members of Parliament are out with their staffs campaigning or supporting their colleagues' campaigns, while those facing retirement are making farewell tours or attending congratulatory dinners, who is representing us in Ottawa? I never thought auditions for a new job should be held on company time.

When will our politicians start to shine? We have made them into stars. Their pictures are on every front page while TV and radio have recorded every move and spoken word. They have performed on stages across the country, been interviewed on the talk shows and willingly posed for the cameras in a wash of publicity greater than that afforded any sport celebrity or movie idol, yet have failed to stir our emotions. If they are worthy of all this attention they should shine. Or at least twinkle a bit.

Are the memorable phrases all used up? I'm not asking for "Give me liberty or give me death," "With malice toward none," or even "Ask not what your country can do for you," but surely our modern politicians can come up with something more pithy than boring inanities about the deficit.

Where are our proud patriots? Like those who said "The twentieth century belongs to Canada" (Laurier), "There are great interests against us, national and international, but the people of Canada have an appointment with destiny" (Diefenbaker), "It is for all to remember that justice is the common concern of mankind" (Mackenzie King).

Where are the statements of commitment to minorities? "I shall grab the instruments of the white man's success, his education, his skills, and with these new tools I shall build my race into the proudest segment of your society" (Chief Dan George). "I have nothing left but my heart, and I gave it long ago to my country" (Louis Riel).

And where is the sense of humour? When asked, "What do you know about agriculture? You're not a farmer," Tommy Douglas replied, "I never laid an egg either, but I know more about making an omelette than a hen does."

I suspect that perhaps our candidates may well be able to turn an apt phrase but are afraid it will come back to haunt them. So every speech is prepared, rehearsed and strained through the nervous eyes of campaign managers, damage control officers, spin doctors and public relations staff. It is then analysed by the media and bounced off the public by opinion pollsters. What is left is tired, safe, humourless and eminently forgettable.

I guess we will not be hearing speeches that soar, rich with imagery, eloquent with poetry that stirs the heart or fires the mind with purpose. Our contenders to high office appear to rely on mundane phrases packaged into sound bites to fit the evening newscast.

How then shall we choose? To avoid merely picking the winner of a popularity contest, we will have to listen and watch diligently for a feeling of competence, a glimmer of foresight, a sense of wisdom.

"If your delight be then in thrones and sceptres, O ye kings of the people, honour wisdom, that ye may reign for evermore."

While I'd like to see succinct expression by our politicians, I would happily do without some of the vicious political rhetoric the U.S. television networks have been bringing into my home.

The Attack of the Religious Right
OCTOBER 1994

I don't suppose there has ever been a leader of a country that hasn't had to face some kind of strong criticism. No matter how conscientiously a prime minister or president tries to govern, certain citizens are going to find fault. This is the nature of the political game and those who aspire to the highest office expect a certain amount of vilification.

Canadians my age can remember the curses aimed at Franklin D. Roosevelt and Mackenzie King, John Diefenbaker and John Kennedy, through Lyndon Johnson, Pierre Trudeau, Richard Nixon and, most recently, Brian Mulroney. They all suffered the slings and arrows of outrageous critics. But I can't remember a more vicious and personal attack on a world leader than is now being experienced by President Bill Clinton.

What is significant about this particular assault on the American leader (and his wife, Hillary) is the fact that it is being organized by Christians. The religious right in the United States is determined to bring the Clintons down and they have the force and the funds to do it.

Part of the anti-Clinton campaign includes the sale of buttons and bumper stickers. Slogans include "AIDS, Abortion, Euthanasia ... Don't Liberals Just Kill Ya?" "Sodom and Gomorrah Had Gays in the Military," "Real Men Are Not Called Hillary" and "Where Is Lee Harvey Oswald When America Really Needs Him?" One booth at the Virginia convention displayed a T-shirt reading "Justice for Clinton." It featured a picture of an aborted fetus. The Reverend Jerry Falwell is using his television program to sell $43 videotapes accusing President Clinton of being involved in murders.

Many thought the evangelical Protestant sects had run out of steam in the late '80s following the conviction of

Jim Bakker for fraud, Jimmy Swaggart's weeping confession of adultery and Pat Robertson's defeat at the polls, but they have rebounded with a vengeance. After Robertson lost, he converted his list of about 2 million names and contacts into an organization called the Christian Coalition. Aided by his expanding commercial and religious empire in Virginia Beach, the coalition spreads its message on numerous television and radio shows and sponsors training seminars on how to take over local political organizations. With over 1.2 million supporters, a current budget of over $20 million and a chapter in every state, the coalition and its allies have had spectacular success this year steamrolling through nomination conventions in Virginia, Texas, Minnesota, Iowa and Kentucky.

In Virginia, supporters of the religious right found their hero as they nominated Oliver North for senator. From the shame of the Iran-Contra scandal to the role of "Christian Soldier," North is being hailed as a future presidential candidate. His supporters, called Prayer Warriors, are provided with instruction sheets that state "prayer and submission to the Father's will and His guidance are the key to victory for Ollie" and include a "program" that involves reading from Psalm 84: "Behold, O God our shield, and look upon the face of Your anointed."

Any pretence at a division between church and state has been abandoned. The coalition's newspaper, *The Christian American*, recruiting for its activist training school, urges,

"Think like Jesus, lead like Moses, fight like David, run like Lincoln."

If this were just the-religious-right-against-the-secular-left kind of battle it might be understandable. It's the virulent and abusive form the campaign is taking that I find so reprehensible.

It's an all-out attack on the president, his wife and the administration. I know that dirty tricks are common to political campaigns, but I never thought I would see them played by the Christian church.

The Search for Ideals in a Dubious Business
AUGUST 1991

Being a politician is likely the most unpopular profession in our country these days. Public opinion polls show them to be only a few notches above cat burglars in garnering our trust and respect. In the United States, it is still the dream of many children to grow up to be president. It would be hard to find a sandbox full of Canadian kids today who have ambitions to be called prime minister.

To serve our country in the political arena should be one of life's finer pursuits. Instead, for idealistic Canadians, it has become a one-way street to ridicule, disillusionment and shattered dreams. Consequently, we tend to be governed by many who seek power for other, less noble reasons — namely self-aggrandizement, personal profit or celebrity status.

While we have some fine elected representatives at both the provincial and federal levels, representing all political parties, they seem to be voices crying from the wilderness of backbenches or smothered by the strictures of caucus.

We are often bewildered when we see the person in whom we have placed our trust on election day dodging important issues, voting with the herd and bending whatever principle is necessary to hold on to power. The taxpayer is not the only one victimized by politicians of this stripe. Consider the beleaguered civil servant.

I was involved for a number of months in a government task force set up under the chairmanship of recently retired auditor-general Kenneth Dye. It was formed to study the value system and ethical stance of Canada's civil service. The report pointed out the multitude of difficulties our government employees face as they try to meet their individual responsibilities to the people who pay their salaries and to the elected officials who hire them.

My colleagues and I learned a lot. We learned that it isn't easy when your primary job is to protect the boss. Over and over again we heard frustrated employees say, "No matter what happens, what foul-ups occur, no blame must be attached to the minister." We learned how working under the strain of shouldering someone else's blunders destroyed morale, creativity, innovation and pride.

I came away from the task-force experience with a great deal of sympathy and respect for a body of people who are trying to do their very best in the field of government service. I also felt shame for senior politicians who seem to be more concerned about the next election and portraying an unsullied image to their constituents than they are about the needs of the country.

I had a call recently from a well-known Canadian figure who asked if I could help him assemble a team of selfless, committed and concerned men and women known for their integrity and dedication to run for federal office in an attempt to bring stability and honour to our political system. Several names came to mind. Many he had already approached. Their responses had been similar. "Who needs the frustration?" Or, "I believe I can do more for a country in my own private way than I can by getting lost in the bureaucratic Ottawa jungle."

While I can sympathize with their feelings, I am reminded of two pertinent quotations. In the eighteenth century, Edmund Burke delivered his immortal observation, "The only thing necessary for the triumph of evil is for good men to do nothing." Of more recent vintage is American Senator Sam Ervin's statement: "If men and women of capacity refuse to take part in politics and government, they condemn themselves, as well as the people, to the punishment of living under bad government."

The challenge is to find people of high ideals who are capable of maintaining them in the capital pressure cooker.

Do Cynical Voters Mean Cynical Politicians?

APRIL 1996

In 1811, philosopher Joseph de Maistre wrote in *Letter to X*, "Every nation has the government it deserves." I guess that means we can only blame ourselves when our chosen few go awry.

I say "awry" because most candidates for public office begin with the sincere intention of serving the country, changing the system for the better and possibly leaving honourable footprints in the political sands of time. But often it seems the person next to whose name we put our confident *X* when voting acts differently once elected. In public speeches he says things like "Women on welfare don't need daycare centres," or she is quoted in the press as being "in favour of gambling casinos that can shave millions off the provincial debt." In caucus with other defenders of party policy, they embrace the expedient, the popular and the trite. Sometimes we never hear at all from the people we elect. It seems as if they have slipped into some dark hole in Ottawa or our provincial capital and can't find their way out.

So I ask myself, Am I getting the government I deserve? Perhaps I am, but I am not getting the government I want and apparently neither are many other Canadians. Opinion polls clearly show that we are dissatisfied. A recent one places politicians at the bottom of the list in the areas of respect and trust. Maybe we expect too much of them, yet they promised us a lot when they were asking for our vote. They said they had new ideas on how to get back to work; they said they were going to set a new course for our country; they said they cared about the young and the old.

They never mentioned they were going to make it almost impossible to get an education. They never shared with us their plan to cut seniors' pensions. Is it any wonder we've become cynical?

When I look back over the years at politicians I have known, there are several who stand out as honourable, hard-working, dedicated and compassionate. That, however, would only be my opinion, and if I were to list them here I'm sure I would elicit a flood of counter-views.

Some politicians are as cynical as the public seems to be. I heard John Crosbie, former MP and Cabinet minister from Newfoundland, tell a TV interviewer a few weeks ago that politics was a "mug's" game. "There are only two reasons to go into politics. If you have the [seat] out of your pants, so poor you can't do anything else, then politics may make you better off than you are. Or, if you are very rich then it doesn't matter, you can spend all the money you need to stay elected."

A very different view comes from Claude Ryan, the man often called "the conscience of Quebec." When I asked him why he ran for office he answered, "I think every person has to answer a few calls in life. Some human beings are privileged to see that call very, very clearly. In my case it came so clear that if I was a man of courage I had to answer the call. But once you've done that you are as you were before. You're no better. But you have a kind of calm that suits your usefulness to the society in which you live. You make a total commitment, then do the best you can."

Recently I invited former governor-general Ed Schreyer to speak to my journalism students at the University of Regina. They asked him why politicians have such a bad reputation. "It is because the media generalizes," he said. "You in journalism need to be more specific. Yes, there are individual politicians who deserve to be criticized, but the majority are doing the very best they can, serving their constituents to the best of their ability. They should be singled out for attention and not included in a cursory dismissal of politicians generally."

Since Schreyer and Ryan are two I would put on my list of dedicated Canadians, I'll pay attention to what they say. I just wish we had more of them.

Perhaps the only things more unpopular than politicians are the taxes they impose on their voters.

Tax Time Seems to Be All the Time
APRIL 1994

In a letter to a friend in 1789, Benjamin Franklin observed,

"In this world nothing is certain but death and taxes." Those of us who haven't experienced the former will certainly have to deal with the latter.

Joseph, the interpreter of dreams in Genesis, is considered to be the first tax collector. Around 700 B.C., he advised Pharaoh to collect one-fifth of the produce in the seven good years to stock up in preparation of the seven bad years to follow. This seemed like such a good idea at the time that Pharaoh gave the job of overseeing this taxation to the 30-year-old Joseph.

By the third century B.C., Rome was into taxation in a big way — auctioning off contracts to allow for tax collection and charging for the use of public works and property. Only in time of war were the citizens taxed directly and then this was returned to them from the spoils captured following the conflict.

In the days preceding the American Revolutionary War, the phrase "Taxation without representation is tyranny" was coined to reject the idea that the British Parliament should be taxing the colonies. It has been pointed out that the Americans did not really want representation, they wanted to do the taxing themselves.

In 1867 the BNA Act gave Canada's Parliament unlimited taxing power. However, for about 50 years, customs and excise duties formed the bulk of the revenue. The provinces got along nicely on fees from licences, permits and sales of commodities or services. Personal income tax was introduced in 1917 to help finance the First World War. Unlike in Roman times, the money was not given back after the war. In fact, it proved so attractive a means of raising money that by 1920, corporate, manufacturer and sales taxes were added. The provinces then decided to get into the act and before the next war they started collecting corporation, sales and, in all but two, personal income taxes.

Over the years, subsequent governments have devised new and ingenious ways of extracting money from us and are undoubtedly at this very moment dreaming up new ones.

I believe most Canadians are proud of this country and are quite willing to pay for the many benefits we receive by living here. It may very well be that we have the best tax administration system in the world, but I still get confused when I hear about some of the ways our money is spent.

We are told more taxes are needed or senior citizen pensions will have to be cut. Then we read about the exorbitant pension plans amounting into the millions being provided to ex-MPs for the rest of their lives. Subsidized housing and low-rental apartment projects will have to be scrapped for lack of funds. Then we find out we are paying $500,000 a year to rent an empty office building in London, England, and the iron-clad lease runs for 17 more years. We worry about increases in medical coverage and user-pay health schemes, then we learn that in one province alone doctors inappropriately billed the public purse for $6.8 million.

There should be some way to follow tax dollars through the system to find out how they are spent and whether or not the payers approve. The municipality where I live has begun a $1.50-a-bag tax on every bag of garbage over one per week. To me this makes sense. It encourages us to recycle, protects our environment and saves on disposal costs.

Recently, as I was preparing to board a plane at one of our large airports, a chap at a desk held out his hand and said, "There is a $10 embarkation tax." Being a law-abiding and authority-intimidated Canadian I gave him the money. Later, on the plane, I wondered. Where will that $10 go? Will it make my flight safer? Will the meal be more digestible? Will it help the airport find my lost luggage? Or, like so many other untraced tax dollars, will it eventually show up in some executive's perks or more free booze in first class?

A Common-Sense Economic Blueprint
APRIL 1991

I am the last person who should ever offer advice on financial matters. My wife, Jane, looks after all our receipts, expenditures, banking, cheque writing and penny pinching. I'm not even sure what she makes or, indeed, what I make. I just know that money comes into our home and goes back out in a seemingly orderly fashion thanks to her realization that "Roy just doesn't have a head for figures."

I found this out when I started earning a weekly pay cheque. I used to cash the cheque, stuff the money in my pants pocket, dole it out until it was gone, then did without until next pay day. When I got married and had the responsibilities of a family, I did what millions of other families did, set up a budget. This was a shoebox full of envelopes individually labelled Groceries, Rent, Fuel, Clothes, Dentist, etc., and every Friday afternoon the cashed cheque was carefully distributed. There was also an envelope called Special where, if possible, a dollar or two collected until we could afford a movie, or a restaurant meal. For many years that envelope saw very little use.

Debt was what you got into when you wanted to buy a car or a house on your own. These were the only two items where being in debt was acceptable and required another envelope for Interest Payments.

Later on, of course, things got more complicated and I had to learn about chequing accounts, mortgage insurance, business expenses, tax credits, tuition fees, union dues and RRSPs, but in financial matters I'm still stuck in that shoebox mentality. In other words, "If you ain't got it, you can't spend it."

Given the fact our government is made up of men and women who must have at one time worked out their own family budget, I don't think it unreasonable to ask that they apply these same principles to the money they have collected from us.

The priorities in the government shoebox seem to be reversed. The housing, food, warmth, education and medical expenses envelopes are being pushed aside in favour of a fatter Special one. This is the envelope that provides funds for political pay-offs, refurbished living quarters, jet-set travel, war toys, golden handshakes and the useless public opinion polls.

In my family budget you only went into debt when your income assured that you could pay it off, plus interest, in a reasonable length of time. Our government has borrowed $380 billion and is having trouble paying $40 billion a year in interest without borrowing more. In order to do this, interest rates are raised to encourage the rich to buy more government bonds, which at the same time dips into the envelopes of the poor and middle-class Canadians who are struggling to meet their mortgage, rent or car payments.

In this country, the only people who became better off were the 20 per cent of the population who belong in the high-income category, that is, the people who make over $64,000 a year and are able to invest, buy bonds, speculate and generally take advantage of the government-controlled high interest rates.

A vast number of Canadians are going broke. Bankruptcies abound. Millions are out of work. We are in the midst of a severe recession that is hurting lower-class families the most. We have almost gotten used to phrases such as "working poor," "food banks" and "street kids." We have managed to hang on to the provincial medical plans and the federal pension system, but we are constantly reminded that both are going broke and that we will have to find the means for increasing our contributions. Why don't the numbers, once touted as reasonable, add up?

While I may not have a "head for figures" and my financial acumen could certainly be considered naive, common sense indicates that the government shoebox could stand a major reshuffling.

Apparently, I'm not the only one who thinks like this.

Do We Face an Anti-Seniors Backlash?
AUGUST 1995

A lot of Canadians entering their senior years are thinking about baby boomers, pension plans, federal deficits and ageism ... and getting very worried.

It's likely that support plans for the elderly will be restructured in the next federal budget. It almost happened last February but politicians backed down at the last minute fearing a "grey power" revolt. Talk of "graduated" old age pensions, clawbacks and the raising of the retirement age is heard constantly on Parliament Hill, as the reality of the situation slowly sinks in.

For years, social policy experts have been warning that Canada faces a seniors crisis as baby boomers reach retirement age. We have also known that because Canadians are living longer, the chance of surviving to old age has increased for everyone. Nine out of every ten of us will reach 65. Two-thirds of these will reach 70 and 40 per cent will reach 75. Of all the massive social changes in this last part of the twentieth century, this is undoubtedly the most profound, but there is little evidence that many of our elected representatives were blessed with the gift of foresight. Perhaps since their pensions are so large and secure the problem never crossed their minds.

Even greater than the financial concern is the increasingly negative attitude I seem to sense toward the old. It's called ageism. We tend to discard the elderly whenever we can. Compulsory retirement and age discrimination in employment are some of the manifestations of ageism. Disregard for the special interests of aged voters by politicians and of aged consumers by business and advertising are additional examples.

Although ageism is cited as a major social problem along with sexism and racism, it is considerably different. Those who are racist or sexist have the luxury of knowing that they will never become members of the group they downgrade. This is not true with ageism. As a matter of fact, we all aspire to become members of the aged group.

The mass media have played a role in our attitudes toward the aged. Most of our advertising is youth-oriented. Intergenerational relations are often portrayed as tenuous and hostile. Some sociologists feel that a de-emphasis of tradition and religion worsens the condition, but, whatever the reason, stereotypes and common misconceptions about the aged are held as truth in our society.

An age bias has even been shown by members of various "helping" professions such as counsellors, psychologists and social workers. Most prefer to work with the young. Even medical students, nurses and doctors consider geriatrics to be one of the least desirable areas of specialization.

With growing public concern regarding economic issues, with the job scare now gripping our country, with a smaller-sized working generation of young people resenting their hard-earned dollars going into old pockets, ageism will flourish and grow.

I hope the "grey power" groups and the government can find a way to work out a solution soon. There is enough hostility in the world now without us starting to hate our elders.

6

ON THE AIR

*"The speed of communications is wondrous
to behold. It is also true that speed can
multiply the distribution of information
that we know to be untrue. The most
sophisticated satellite has no conscience."*

— EDWARD R. MURROW, *"FAMILY OF
MAN" SPEECH*

Violence in Society? Don't Blame TV
JULY 1994

Almost everyone is concerned about violence in our society and whenever it is discussed you will hear "the media"
come in for the largest share of blame.

At a recent seminar on violence in the media, I tried to discover what the participants meant as they waxed eloquently on this subject. It turned out they did not mean newspapers, which only report stories of violence as they cover crime news. Radio is not suspect since it has evolved into a kind of Muzak with commercials. Magazines and periodicals don't apparently incite us to any emotion, so that leaves television. Indeed, when people talk about media in relation to violence, television is what they are targetting.

Our federal government, always on the alert for a politically advantageous hobby horse, has turned its attention to this subject, possibly as a means of diverting our attention from more pressing concerns, but also because they know very well they won't have to do anything about it. The fact is, there is very little they can do.

Our justice minister, the heritage minister, the head of the Canadian Radio-television and Telecommunications Commission (CRTC) are all "viewing with alarm" the amount of violence shown on television, but it would be more helpful if they revealed just what programs it is they are viewing. Certainly not Canadian ones. With the possible exception of *Hockey Night in Canada*, we simply do not produce "violent" programs. What little programming we do manage to package and distribute is more along the lines of *Road to Avonlea* or *Mr. Dressup*. *Question Period* gets fairly raucous at times; perhaps this is where we could improve.

What they and other concerned Canadians are talking

about, of course, are the American cop dramas, purulent public affairs infotainment shows, some sitcoms and cartoons. There is no doubt that hours of gratuitous violence flow across the border daily, but our federal watchdogs know full well there is no way they can influence what U.S. television networks broadcast.

Last year, an all-party committee of MPs warned the broadcast industry to start doing a better job of "policing what Canadians watch on TV or brace for the prospect of federal intervention." Unless the lawmakers have discovered some way of banning the big U.S. networks or influencing the Federal Communications Commission, these are empty words indeed. If memory serves, it was the CRTC, not so long ago, that was making such a show of granting licences to cable companies for the express purpose of assuring that all Canadians would have access to American programs.

Pierre Trudeau once said, "The state has no place in the bedrooms of the nation." Surely that holds true for the living rooms as well. Canadians have always watched more American programming than our own. This will not change and it will increase as individual satellite dishes remove all international boundaries.

If we are convinced that television is such a large factor in encouraging violence we can: (1) stop watching certain shows; (2) write protest letters to networks and producers; (3) boycott the products advertised on these shows and let the sponsor know we are doing it.

If we suspect that the major causes of violence in our society are unemployment, poverty, bad housing, hunger, drugs, illiteracy, lack of support services or 101 other obvious reasons, perhaps then our leaders can make a worthwhile contribution to the problem.

Blaming television is too easy and non-productive.

As Henry David Thoreau said, "There are a thousand hacking at the branches of evil to one who is striking at the root."

Three Words in Favour of Public Broadcasting in Canada: *As It Happens*
JULY 1995

If you are looking for intelligent, non-violent broadcasting, you might do well to turn off your TV and turn on the radio.

To me, radio has always seemed to be the ideal medium of information and entertainment. It does not hold you captive; you can do other things while you listen. It's the perfect companion while you drive, do household chores, read, lie on the beach, jog or mow the lawn. It was an exciting part of my young life, bringing a world of music, drama and comedy to our remote farm community. Later on I chose it as a career and spent 15 years exploring every facet of the business.

Radio today bears little resemblance to what I experienced in the days when we actually produced programs that had a beginning and an end, or delivered in-depth newscasts instead of merely headlines. It has become, in the private sector, a commercial machine desperately trying to attract a fragmented audience with an array of trite, boring formats. A recent ruling by the CRTC allowing stations to switch programming policy without prior permission will only add to the confusion.

Stations that used to introduce new music in what was called the Top-Forty format found their audience drifting away to more familiar material. The Golden Oldies approach takes us as far back as the Beatles. (I find it interesting that Nostalgia TV means Chaplin and Garbo. Nostalgia Radio means Bob Dylan.) Talk radio is springing up in some major centres but relies far too much on open-line segments, which deteriorate rapidly into exchanges of ignorance. Country stations that thrived a few years ago featuring Kenny Rogers, Dolly Parton and John Denver have returned to the "hurtin' and cryin' " tunes that even make the commercials sound depressing. Have you heard "I'm Mixed Up in Mexico, Living on Refried Dreams"?

The industry is not doing well. Last year very few Canadian radio stations showed a profit. Many are turning to automation as a means of cutting out salaried employees. Some stations simply download a satellite feed, which allows insertion of pre-programmed commercials and the dispensing of staff altogether.

That leaves us with public radio. Fortunately, CBC remembers why the medium was invented. With Gzowski in the morning, Gabereau in the afternoon, *As It Happens* in the evening and *Ideas* at night, plus the incomparable programming on CBC Stereo with its preference for our own classical artists and composers, Canadians have the best radio service in the world.

When President Clinton addressed the House of Commons in 1995, I was surprised to hear him say how much Americans appreciated the CBC. Then I remembered that *As It Happens* is carried on the U.S. Public Radio network. Without a doubt, it is the most compelling and listenable program on the air today. It covers the top news stories by bringing us the people involved. It explores current issues with throroughness and originality. Michael Enright and Barbara Budd provide a serious, compassionate and sometimes humorous balance that leaves the listener glad to have spent an hour and a half in their company. Back Porch Al (or Fireplace Al, depending on the season) still returns once in a while to give us the remarkable storytelling talents of Alan Maitland. With the added feature of the call-back machine, listeners can respond to previous items, adding personal and often illuminating views.

True communication has been described in terms of a circle. The information goes out, is digested, reacted to, then returned to the sender. This is what makes *As It Happens* the quintessential radio program.

The CBC is threatened with more cuts to its budget. It can't survive much more. There are those who would privatize the public network. I would suggest these people listen to *As It Happens* for a few evenings and ask themselves if it would ever be duplicated in the commercial marketplace.

If As It Happens *is the best example of the broad circle of communications, surely video games are the worst example of an ever-tightening element of that same circle. There, a cycle of violence is replayed over and over, right in our own living rooms.*

Controlling the Spread of Objectionable Children's Games
JANUARY 1995

If anyone at your house received or purchased a video game it may have had a warning label on the package. Responding to concerns expressed by parents and government, the Canadian Interactive Digital Software Association announced in November 1994 that henceforth their products would be rated according to the amount of sex, graphic violence and foul language they contained.

This is a good idea as far as it goes. For some time, I have felt the industry was irresponsible and insensitive to the rising concern most of us have about the increasingly violent and pornographic game market. The ratings are as follows: Early Childhood (age 3 and over) — no violence. Kids (age 6+) — scenes of mild animated violence. Teen (age 13+) — contains all of the above plus animated blood and gore and mild language with words like *damn* or *hell.* Mature (age 17+) — this category may contain everything in Teen plus realistic blood and gore, strong four-letter language, use of drugs and sexual innuendo. Adults Only would contain graphic sex in addition to everything in the Mature category.

Some games were rated before the '94 holiday season, some weren't. For example, the very popular Mortal Kombat II, where the name of the game is to rip out the heart or spinal cord of your opponent, is already in thousands of Canadian homes. The game Night Trap has been on the market for years with no rating attached. It was among the first games to use video of real actors. In one scene, three ghouls use a blood-draining auger to kill a woman in a negligee. It is horrifying because of its sexual innuendoes and violence toward women.

Despite the industry's assurance that they can best decide what levels of violence are appropriate to every age group, many people, myself included, still have concerns about the entire home-game market. Rose Dyson, chairperson of Canadians Concerned About Violence in Entertainment, says, "A warning label is likely to spark interest in the youngsters. Kids like to emulate their elders. Excessive exposure to violence — whether on television or computer screens — leads children to hyperactivity, lack of concentration, anxiety and a feeling that violence is the best resolution for problems."

Computer Gaming World editor John Wilson says, "Letting game companies lead the way is a mistake. It continues the almost-mythology that games are simply for kids." Wilson, whose magazine's average reader is 30 years old, adds, "I fail to see how predominantly video-game companies can speak for the whole industry."

He has a good point. We're not just talking video games here. What about the games on cartridges, CDs and floppy disks, as well as those available by modem from on-line services, tomorrow's interactive cable games and others not yet conceived?

It would be almost impossible to have an independent panel rate video games considering the many hours it would take to work through the various levels of even the simple ones, plus the fact that more than 1,000 games are released each year. Comparatively, a movie industry review board handles only about 600 titles a year.

In the Canadian Interactive Digital Software Association announcement there was no mention of any penalty for dealers who sold the adult-rated games to children. Perhaps the fact that these games cost between $60 and $90 leads them to assume that most are being purchased by adults.

I urge parents to realize that if they allow this violent and sexually explicit material into the home, the kids will find it and use it — the same as they do with television programs or magazines that are rated "for adults only."

Of course, television has been around much longer and its negative aspects are far more insidious than those of the video games.

Television on the Cheap
MARCH 1994

Television, the medium that used to provide well-crafted drama starring talented performers or variety hours with superb musicians, singers and dancers, has relinquished any pretence of creativity in favour of the unprofessional and the unaccomplished. Increasingly, our television hours are filled with the antics of show-business wannabes. It's becoming difficult to watch for an entire evening without the feeling that our major networks have been taken over by a local amateur night.

Programs such as *America's Funniest Home Videos* pay viewers to send them shots of their children, friends or pets in contrived and often cruel situations as fodder for a giggling laugh track. Programs like *Rescue 911*, *Cops* and *Unsolved Mysteries* purport to mirror "real-life situations" as they simulate incidents of tragedy and anguish using the people involved as props in tacky melodramas.

On some networks, daytime drama is being forced off the air by the mushrooming number of talk shows that parade a string of misfits ostensibly to interact with a well-rehearsed studio audience. While I have never been a fan of the soap opera format, at least they use writers, actors and creative minds. The current audience-participation talk programs have tapped the voyeuristic tendencies of the kind of people we used to see lined up at the "freak" tent in the midway of our county fairs. Promotions for these programs imitate the barker's cry: "Tomorrow on *Geraldo*, see women who married devil worshippers and the demons they spawned." The new twist is that a studio audience is encouraged to participate by challenging the guests and the host verbally, and sometimes physically, to the amusement of the home viewer.

The networks defend the trend as a democratizing of the medium. Now, they tell us, "ordinary people" are having their say. How noble. How fallacious.

More shows are built around gullible hoi polloi because it is the cheapest way to fill the hours of programming. Talent costs money. Today in television, the dollar is indeed almighty. The lower the production budget, the sooner the show becomes part of the schedule. The sleazier and more salacious the topic, the better the chance of snaring the undiscriminating couch potato. If they can find a "hot" property (say, Rush Limbaugh), package his open-line program (the cheapest format in broadcasting) and let him spill his racist venom from coast to coast, they've got a ratings winner and a high profit margin.

There was a time when advertisers like General Motors, Kraft or Hallmark provided the money to hire writers like Rod Serling, Paddy Chayefsky and Gore Vidal to script material for actors such as Rod Steiger, Joanne Woodward or Ernest Borgnine. Anything like that today would not be regarded as "cost efficient." The hours of music by fine musicians, dancers and singers is fading from the airwaves. With very few exceptions our current crop of comedians fail to evoke laughter unless one is amused by sexual innuendo or coarse language. A stand-up comic routine about bodily functions costs very little to produce.

We know what is happening on the technical side of television: personal satellite dishes the size of dinner plates, digital video compression expanding 60 channels to 200, telecomputers allowing us access to an electronic superhighway where we can call up thousands of programming and non-progamming services. But what we don't know is what will be out there worth calling up. As the advertising dollar is more thinly spread, talent and creativity will continue to suffer. You don't need screenplays for unscripted programs. You don't need musicians for sound effects. You don't need actors for "reality" programs.

As one television critic recently commented, "If we are

all behind the curtain working the controls like the Wizard of Oz, there'll be no Dorothy left to dazzle."

When Pictures Move for Profit
MAY 1993

It was almost 90 years ago that the first major movie was seen and appreciated by the public. It could have been earlier, but Thomas Edison considered his invention of the kinetoscope merely a curiosity and spent much more time on his electrical experiments.

Only after competitors began using his invention to make clips such as a man walking his dog, a balloon floating in the air or a train arriving at a station, did the "Wizard of Menlo Park" realize he had something important and decide to patent the process. The moving picture industry was further delayed by numerous court manoeuvres.

It was a French stage magician named Georges Méliès who developed what we now call special effects. Though crude at the time, techniques such as fades, dissolves, stop motion and the simple idea of telling a story gave birth to a whole new medium of communication. But it was one of Edison's camera operators, Edwin S. Porter, who came up with the idea of a full-length feature with characters the audience could boo, hiss or cheer.

The Great Train Robbery was the first movie to work from a script, the first to hire professional actors and the first to spawn a real movie star, Max Aronson, who went on to become "Broncho Billy." It was only 14 minutes in length but swept the continent, beginning the movie industry as we know it today.

It also established another profession — the movie critic. The *Philadelphia Inquirer* of June 26, 1904, wrote, "There is a great amount of shooting. The smoke from the pistols can be plainly seen and men drop dead right and left. In the pursuit of the sheriff one is shot in the back and the way in which he tumbles from his horse and strikes the ground leaves the spectator wondering if he is not a dummy, for it does not seem possible that a man could take such a fall and live."

So for the first time we find people wondering what is real and what is phoney when pictures move for profit. Over the years, we came to accept the fact that going to the movies meant entering a world of make-believe. Part of the reason for our love of the big screen was that it gave us a chance to escape from the real world. The sheer size of the image in front of us allowed us to suspend our disbelief. The characters we saw and the scenes in which they were set could not be compared to our own lives.

When the screen became smaller and came into our living room by way of a medium called television, I think we expected something different. This was more personal. Our relationship to the images was closer and we were constantly asked to believe what we saw.

News was presented as fact. Commercials told us that a product "really, really worked." Drama was produced as a "slice of life" featuring people "just like you." Sitcoms took place in kitchens and bedrooms the same as ours.

Critics still warned us, however, that the pictures lied. We were being manipulated as surely as we were in *The Great Train Robbery*, only with more sophistication. Many times, when I spoke in schools or held "How to Watch TV" seminars for young people, I would be censured by teachers and parents for trying to turn children into cynics. I usually countered with the argument that I was trying to make them sceptics. The difference? A sceptic is one who questions the validity of something that is said to be true. A cynic is a person who believes that only selfishness motivates human action.

What are we now to make of these moving images that take up such a large part of our lives? When we learn that battle scenes from real wars have been staged for the camera, when a jury panel can watch a video of a man being beaten and say that it didn't happen, when we watch deceased movie stars like Humphrey Bogart, James Cagney and Cary Grant sell Diet Coke, are we not tempted to move from scepticism to cynicism?

It seems we must now all become critics. We will have to judge what we see on a case-by-case basis. We are forced to separate what we realize is done with creative licence for entertainment or dramatic effect, from what we suspect is done solely to lie for profit. Perhaps we need to become both sceptic and cynic as we sift the counterfeit from the correct to distinguish what is worth noting and what is worth nothing.

I'm sure when people left the theatre after *The Great Train Robbery*, they must have exclaimed, "My, a picture is indeed worth a thousand words!" Now are we not entitled to ask if the picture we see is worth even one word?

Bean-Counters Rule the Airwaves
NOVEMBER 1992

If you're still watching North American television, you've likely noticed more confusion than usual. This is because, in a desperate bid for ratings in an incredibly fragmented market, broadcast executives are grasping at any straw in the Hertzian wind. Three obvious trends are in evidence this fall.

First, the grab for the young viewer. Last summer the youth-oriented, often irreverent Fox network quickly jumped over the sleeping NBC, CBS and ABC while they were covering political conventions, and landed in first place for the only time in its eight-year existence. This resulted in a follow-the-leader decision by the big three. To be fair, CBS is trying to split its focus by including a handful of shows aimed at an older audience who, according to their pollsters, still have control of the purse strings. ABC and NBC have made no bones about their quest for younger viewers, and their new programs reflect that intention.

They are blatant copies of *Married ... with Children*, *In Living Color*, *Beverly Hills 90210* and *The Simpsons*. Since Canadian viewers have access to all the new American programs, either beamed across the border or actually carried by our own networks, it's becoming difficult for the adult mind to enjoy an evening of stimulating fare.

Canadian producers too are concerned with age demographics. The CBC claims that its news audience, traditionally made up of older viewers, is now going to bed earlier. They have therefore moved *The National* back to 9 p.m. They have also cancelled *The Journal*, the finest in-depth current affairs program on either side of the border. The administration has relinquished all programming decisions to the entertainment department.

Second, the focus on sex. Most of the new sitcoms are deliberately oriented toward more blatant sexual relationships. To cite an example, in its opener, the *Love and War* protagonists, having just met, discuss whose supply of condoms is the most fashionable. Executive producer Diane English, creator of *Murphy Brown*, explains. "There are no children on this show. These people aren't married. Family values are not a priority." The show, however, does air at traditional family viewing time. One reviewer has summed up this season's offering of situation comedies as "Prime Time Lust."

Third, the "reality" shows. These are the programs that encourage you to be an armchair cop by phoning toll-free numbers with tips to catch everyone from serial killers to bank robbers.

Because programs such as *America's Most Wanted, Unsolved Mysteries* and *Top Cops* were such ratings-grabbers last year, they have been joined by a half dozen clones for the new season. Why are they so popular? One psychology professor says, "With a battered economy and general social malaise, people have a feeling they've lost control of their lives. These shows give people a sense they have control, whether it's realistic or not." Other psychologists and criminologists claim the shows are overly violent, give a false image of crime solving, desensitize the viewer and trivialize the victim's suffering.

The trend at both the private and public broadcasting networks is clear. The artistic and creative people in the medium — the quality producers, directors and writers — are being replaced by the bean-counters and business suits whose only aim is to get greater hype, higher ratings and of course more money.

I have some suggestions for the concerned viewer. Be selective. Read the listings in advance and decide what you will watch; too often the television set is just left on like another public utility. Use your VCR to tape quality programs for more convenient viewing; no programmer knows your habits. Watch the programs with other family members and discuss the content during and after. This can ameliorate any damage to sensitive ears and give you fodder for discussions about societal trends and how your family fits in. Write a critique of what you see and send your praise or objections to the network and the sponsor. It doesn't always work if a program is popular enough, but they do listen.

Of course, there is always a last alternative called the Off button.

Sleazy Television Goes Mainstream
SEPTEMBER 1990

Despite the influence of bean-counters, we are told by our network executives that today's television is coming of age. This sounds like a good idea for those of us who have claimed over the years that it was aimed generally for the ten-year-old intelligence, but I think our broadcasting czars are confusing excellence with "X" ratings.

For a person my age who remembers when Ricky and Lucy had to sleep in separate beds and Barbara Eden had to cover up her navel in *I Dream of Jeannie*, the medium has matured a tad too much. Prime-time television is routinely going where previous standards of good taste never allowed it to go. In an effort to compete with racier cable programming, pay-per-view channels and video rentals, the major U.S. networks are churning out steamy material at an increasing rate.

Leading the way is the Fox network. Many pundits did not give the fledgling network a chance to survive and they seemed to be right for the first two seasons. Then programmers at Fox got the bright idea to challenge existing values on a weekly basis. They created two highly successful yet exceedingly controversial comedies: first, *Married ... with Children*, then *The Simpsons*. *Married ... with Children* routinely jiggles its way through plots that centre on an inane, rude father, a vacuous, sex-charged mother, a voyeuristic son and a nymphomaniac daughter. Redeeming social or artistic value does not even enter the picture. *The Simpsons*, though not sexually explicit, extols the virtue of being marginally intelligent. One ep. ode debated whether father Homer Simpson was indeed a member of the human race or a vegetable. No one seemed particularly concerned either way. Both shows garner healthy ratings.

We've become used to the topics of daytime talk shows. One broadcasting critic said recently, "If you think *Geraldo*, *Donahue* and *Oprah* are dealing with kinky subjects now, in a few years these current programs will seem as bland as *Mr. Rogers Neighborhood*.

One also notes that the networks have slashed their standards and practices departments, which monitor excesses. Matthew Morgo, who was CBS vice-president of standards and practices, says, "These changes are pushing the boundaries further." His NBC counterpart says, "We are in a different business today. We try to be more in the mainstream." It is worrisome to believe that the mainstream is defined in such blatantly prurient, banal terms.

Some viewers were concerned a few years ago when their favourite afternoon soap operas took on a much racier tone. Not too much fuss was made, however, since they weren't in prime time and the younger members of the family were in school. The soaps have since actually mellowed somewhat, citing the AIDS scare as reason for soft-pedalling the more explicit sexual scenes.

The so-called public affairs programs have not escaped this trend. *A Current Affair, Rescue 911* and many others of this ilk emphasize the sensational side of the news, use re-creations constantly and purport to be informing the public. Many polls show that in fact the audience for these programs believes the content unquestionably and counts watching them in the same category as reading a newspaper.

Where will it end? Well, the answer to that is obvious. It will end only when the viewer gets up, walks over to the set and shuts it off.

It Starts with *T* — and Stands for Trouble
MAY 1991

Sociologists have told us for some time now that children spend more time watching television that they do in any other activity, except sleeping. They spend more time in front of the TV set than they do in classrooms when you subtract recesses, noon hours and spare periods. Apologists for the medium claim this statement is misleading, since much of television is educational. Whether they watch educational programs or not, I'm concerned with the number of hours that kids spend glued to this mind-numbing box. Two bits of recent information received lately have turned this concern into alarm.

A manufacturer of baby cribs has just announced an innovative new model. In the corner of the crib is a small TV monitor that relays programs selected from the family set and is designed to keep the baby entertained and amused (read: quiet) at any time during the day or night.

In Kansas, some school buses are being equipped with a television set and VCR to keep the kids entertained and amused (read: quiet) while they travel to and from school. In a radio interview, one of the bus drivers praised the system, saying the students "behaved like lambs" as they watched reruns of TV programs.

Clearly we are using television to sedate children. How often have we asked noisy kids, "Why don't you go and watch some TV?" Could it be that television watching contributes to their later restlessness? Like any narcotic, television induces a stuporous lethargy. When it wears off, people become edgy, more rambunctious, more disruptive. A child's natural energy is repressed while lost in TV-land only to explode when the tranquillizer is removed.

Yes, there are programs of educational merit on television, but I don't believe these are the children's favourites. If they were, we would see a more competent group of young people as they get older.

How alarmed am I? Think about this. One in five Canadians 15 years of age or older, most of them born in this country, are unable to read this sentence. They also couldn't read it if it was translated into French. Statistics Canada tells us that about a quarter of young people aged 16 to 24 can manage only simple reading materials for jobs that are "not too complex." Six per cent of young adults cannot read at all and barely recognize key words in common written material.

If all the television sets in the country were shut off, it would not necessarily change those statistics. But surely more time away from the set would give a child the opportunity to assimilate what was taught in school, more time to talk, to think and to ask questions. More time to be creative, to wonder and dream.

In the 1979 movie *Being There*, Peter Sellers plays a man whose every waking hour is spent in front of a television set. All he knows is what he's seen on TV. All he says is what he's heard on TV. At one point he strays out of the house and walks down a very rough street. When confronted with some dangerous characters at a street corner, he points his ever-present TV remote control at them, thinking he can turn them off and make them go away. I see by the papers that reality has caught up with fiction, at least in Southern California. A newspaper reports that Javier Gonzales Alvarado, 29, was shot and killed by police as he aimed what they believed was a pistol. It turned out to be a TV remote tuner.

Witnesses had reported a man standing in an intersection Sunday, aiming what looked like a semi-automatic pistol at passing vehicles, police spokesman Christopher Loop said yesterday.

"His behaviour," Loop said, "led police to believe he was under the influence of drugs."

Putting the Brakes on a Violent Culture
JULY 1991

Despite the smug feelings of many Canadians, senseless violence is not limited to the United States. Canada has about 600 homicides each year. We also have about 25,000 police reports of sexual assault, including those committed against children, and an additional 180,000 assaults of all description.

Our neighbours to the south have four times as many violent crimes per capita as we do. In fact, any country experiencing more violent crimes than the U.S. is likely experiencing civil war. American culture is violent and we share it. The presentation of American life offered in movies, television and video is overwhelmingly savage.

Hideous forms of violence and bodily harm are shown without remorse by the characters portrayed, and their actions are glorified as right and in the name of justice.

We are a society that promotes violence in entertainment. Gulf War videos have been flooding the market. CNN has distributed 300,000 copies of Gulf War tapes through Turner Home Video, just the beginning of a six-part series of censored and sanitized war images showing only the dead bodies of our so-called enemies.

During Saturday-morning children's television, our kids can see an act of brutality every four minutes and a murder every six. By age 18, our children will have seen 200,000 acts of violence and 50,000 murders while watching 20,000 hours of television. Where would the North American entertainment industry be without violence? It sells, it's popular and it makes the consumer feel powerful.

Six out of ten bestselling monthly magazines are classified as "men's entertainment." The combined sales of *Playboy* and *Penthouse* outsell *Time* and *Newsweek*. There are 260 periodicals in the U.S. devoted to child pornography.

Some psychological reports have told us that violent media are not harmful and perhaps even healthy because they provide an outlet for "natural" aggressive tendencies. But other, more recent research studying the effects of media violence and pornography tells us that the "outlet" is the practice of aggression and that they reinforce the behaviour. There is no doubt in my mind that there is a significant connection between North America's violent media vision of life and its high crime rate. Our children are being taught every day that violence is an acceptable method of dealing with difficulties or relieving oneself of uncomfortable feelings.

Real and replica handguns are becoming a status symbol in Canadian high schools. Studies show that today's teen's biggest fear is of gangs of other teenagers. One in five has had a frightening encounter and one in ten has been robbed or assaulted. Marlene Webber, author of *Street Kids*, says frustrated children turn to violence, extortion and robbery because they mimic the morality of the rich and powerful. This morality is glorified in our daily media diet.

I have never been, nor am I now, a supporter of censorship, but surely there is a difference between our ability to select what we read, see or hear and our ability to escape the onslaught of material that is foisted upon us at every push of a button. It is also time that our laws regarding the dissemination of hate literature be enforced to protect us from material that promotes the hatred and degradation of women and children.

Not so long ago in the movies and radio of the '30s and '40s, the racist depiction of North American natives was virtually unnoticed. Antisemitism and black stereotyping were accepted as harmless entertainment. We have made quite a bit of progress in these areas. But when it comes to seeing pornography, violence and sexism as infringements of our human rights, we still have a long way to go.

It's not enough for television to insult our morality; it often insults our intelligence, too.

Ranking the Reporter Ahead of the Subject
JULY–AUGUST 1996

I am finding it very difficult to watch or listen to newscasts any more as a means of actually understanding what is going on. This is because of a new style of journalism I call "What I hear you saying!" This hackneyed phrase was used in the '60s when interviewers were obsessed with getting inside their subjects and examining their "true feelings." It is a kind of reporting that focuses on the journalist or the news reader instead of on the news maker.

News reader: "In Ottawa today Prime Minister Chrétien announced further changes to federal subsidies. Here in our nation's capital is Jason Cobbledick."

Jason: "Thank you, Paul. The prime minister addressed an overflow crowd at the convention centre and emphatically made several points." (*We see Mr. Chrétien waving his arms and shouting to a crowd.*)

Chrétien: "… of utmost importance. Canadians will be

happy to hear ..." (*The camera cuts back to Cobbledick while the prime minister continues talking.*)

Jason: "The PM went on to list ten points that he thought should be followed . . ."

The thinking, apparently, is that the reporter or anchor can present the speaker's words better than the speaker can. Seldom is the speaker, be it politician or witness to an accident, allowed to tell the story themselves. The program producer says, "Cut away here, do an on-camera bit here, wrap up the story here, and get on to the next bit."

No one wants to take precious moments away from the newscast to actually hear the people who make the news. Better to have the announcer paraphrase. It saves time and makes it easier for us not-too-bright viewers to understand.

Sometimes all we see is a picture of the event. In the background, people are talking, likely dropping pearls of wisdom all over the place, but it is the announcer who tells us what was said and what it meant. Straining the news through a surrogate mouthpiece, no matter how well coiffed or glib, is not my idea of getting the real story. We are not getting first-hand accounts of events, we are getting the essence of the news. Sometimes we just get sound effects or prissy editorial assessments by so-called experts brought in to comment on these ludicrous sound bites.

Can you imagine what it would have been like if this kind of journalism had been practised back in the days when Winston Churchill or Franklin D. Roosevelt were making news?

Anchor: "We take you now to the British House of Commons where Prime Minister Winston Churchill is speaking about the Dunkirk evacuation."

Churchill: "We shall not flag or fail. We shall go on to the end. We shall fight in France, we shall fight ..." (*Fade to background.*)

Anchor: "Mr. Churchill continued to describe the places he would suggest fighting. They included the seas and oceans, beaches and landing grounds, fields and streets and indicated that we would never surrender."

Announcer: "Today in a radio broadcast, Prime Minister Churchill urged English citizens to be brave and fight back. He said we should brace ourselves and that if the British Empire lasted for a thousand years this would be our finest hour. We bring you now the sound of the applause that greeted his speech."

Here is how today's reporters would cover President Roosevelt's first inaugural address:

Announcer: "Today in Washington, commenting on the Depression, the president said that the only thing we had to fear was fear itself. Here, commenting on the president's statement, is Professor Crabb from Harvard."

Prof. Crabb: "Thank you for the opportunity to set the record straight. As we all know, that phrase is stolen directly from Henry David Thoreau, who said, 'Nothing is so much to be feared as fear.' However, some of my colleagues would trace it back even further to Montaigne in the 1500s, who said, 'The thing I fear most is fear.' Now, whether this deliberate act of plagiarism will cause a backlash in Congress against our new president remains to be seen. We could very well be facing a Poetrygate here."

If our current crop of journalists were covering King Edward VIII's abdication speech it might go something like this:

Announcer: "We take you now to Windsor Castle."

Edward: "At long last, I am able to say a few words of my own —"

Announcer: "In a halting and emotional statement King Edward spoke directly to his subjects today concluding with the statement that he could not carry out his duties without the so-called help and support of the woman he loves. Details at 11."

Cutbacks to the Future: Remembering the CBC
FEBRUARY 1991

Once upon a time in 2001, a father, mother and five-year-old daughter had just finished their evening meal.

"Shall I see if there is anything to watch on television?" asked Father.

"There's not much point," answered Mother. "It will just be the same American game shows and sitcoms.

Remember when we used to have Canadian dramas and interesting documentaries and music programs? Remember the CBC?"

"What's the CBC?" asked Daughter.

"Well, before you were born, dear, there used to be a network called the Canadian Broadcasting Corporation," explained Father. "All of the citizens of this country chipped in about 11 cents a day, which the government collected in taxes, so that we could have our own programs."

"Who made the programs?" asked Daughter.

"Oh, we had our own producers, actors, writers and camera people. We had broadcasting stations all across the country from Newfoundland to British Columbia. We had programs in French and English and dozens of native languages. Our programs were seen all over the world. Some people said there was no better broadcasting system anywhere on earth."

"My, you are stirring up old memories," said Mother, fondly. "Remember how we would never go to bed without watching *The National* and *The Journal*? The day never seemed complete until Peter and Barbara said goodnight."

"How about *the fifth estate*? There was a show that really got to the bottom of things. Or *Marketplace*? Remember how they used to test new products and warn us about shoddy merchandise?" asked Father.

"Yes, and I'll never forget *Man Alive* and *The Nature of Things*. We learned so much about people who really made a difference in our world and about the wonders of our natural environment," replied Mother.

"Were there also programs for children?" asked Daughter.

"Indeed there were. There were shows called *The Friendly Giant, Mr. Dressup, The Polka-Dot Door* and great dramas like *Anne of Green Gables*," said Father.

"And don't forget the wonderful music programs," chimed in Mother. "I can still see the ballets they used to put on and hear the symphonies. There were pop singers and dancers, country music and jazz ... something for everybody."

"Why did the CBC quit?" asked Daughter.

"Well, it didn't exactly quit, dear," explained Father. "You see, the government didn't like the CBC because it was always telling the truth about what went on in Ottawa, so they gradually took its money away. Soon, there were only American programs, which was fine with the government because they never mentioned Ottawa."

"You see, dear," added Mother, "the government didn't think it was important to link the nation together so that we could see what other people in this country thought or how they lived. It was the same with Via Rail."

"What's Via Rail?" asked Daughter.

"Never mind, dear," said Father. "That's another story. We better get to bed. Tomorrow will be a busy day. We have to pick up Grandma and Grandpa at the airport. They're flying in from Halifax on American Airlines."

*I'm certainly a fan of the CBC, but for many years I
worked in private radio. The last of my radio days were
spent in religious broadcasting.*

Talking about God
MAY 1997

I was cleaning out a corner of the attic the other day when
I came across a box of old correspondence, bills, receipts
and radio scripts dating back to the couple of years my
family and I spent in Vancouver in the '60s. I had taken on
the position of regional director of broadcasting for the
United Church of Canada in British Columbia and while I
could handle the broadcasting end of the job with no problem, I had little expertise in the church part. In those days
the church was very much involved with radio and had
regional directors in various parts of the country. The
responsibilities differed from one district to another but
generally were divided between helping distribute national
programs, forming a link between the media and the
churches, and originating productions. The very popular
Tell Me a Story and *The Nancy Edwards Show* were
regularly distributed, on tape, from Berkeley Studio in
Toronto. The current affairs program *Checkpoint*, which
was produced in conjunction with the Anglican Church of
Canada, was becoming a talked-about addition to the
schedules of nearly 90 stations from coast to coast.

At one time the United Church had owned radio station CKWX in Vancouver. When it was sold to private interests, the church retained four hours a week, and one of the director's jobs was to fill those four hours. Some of the time could be taken up with a nightly devotional show and a morning bulletin board of religious news. The national programs and a Sunday church service took care of the rest. When the contract with the local church for its weekly service expired, we had an empty hour on our hands, and the station pushed for something more innovative and ratings-boosting. It was then I introduced the program *God Talk*.

Open-line radio programs were very popular in Vancouver in the '60s and names like Pat Burns and Jack Webster were household words. So, why not a religious open-line show, one that would answer any question, deal with any issue? And what better title for the show than the subject under discussion? Because I certainly didn't have the qualifications to answer anyone's theological concerns, I assembled a blue-ribbon panel and acted as moderator. And what a group we had! Rev. Art Hives represented the Anglican Church, Father Ed Bader of the Catholic Information Centre gave the Catholic viewpoint and Rev. Jack Shaver, chaplain at University of British Columbia, weighed in for the United Church. From time to time, spokespersons from other denominations and faiths volunteered as guests on the show, and we even involved the odd agnostic and atheist. The audience loved it and the ratings zoomed.

God Talk became a breath of fresh air in an otherwise dull Sunday-morning broadcasting scene. Audiences increased to such an extent that the station's sales department asked if they could sell advertising on it. Some local clergy tried to have its 11-o'clock time slot changed. They had discovered members of their congregations in church listening to *God Talk* on their portable radios with one ear and the sermon with the other.

It was a good-natured program with lots of discussion on ethical and moral issues. My panel members usually agreed, but sometimes a spirited exchange of views would underline denominational differences. What I liked was the fact that listeners felt free to ask questions, simple or profound, that had been bothering them about various elements of faith. We had a segment of the program to answer questions that had been written to us from people who preferred not to go on the air. To my surprise, as I emptied out long-forgotten boxes in my attic I found copies of some of those questions. I wish I could remember what answers my panel gave. Some may sound frivolous now, but believe me they were asked with real sincerity.

"Is it possible for man to live by bread alone? If so, how long?"

"How come there are seven days in the week? Why not eight? It says God rested on the seventh day. Did those days have 24 hours?"

"When I consider that I have two parents, four grand-parents, eight great-grandparents — ancestors doubling in each generation — it eventually amounts to billions going back in time. Genesis tells us that the human race started out with only a few people then steadily increased. What happens when these two surging numerical tides run into each other?"

"Did the Corinthians write back?"

I know these questions are over 30 years old. Quite likely they are older than that.

7

THE LEARNING
GAME

"Education is what you have left over
after you have forgotten everything you
have learned."

— OLD SAYING

The World's Gentlest Reviewer
SEPTEMBER 1993

I have always enjoyed reading reviews of new artistic creations. Newspapers and magazines featuring book or theatre criticism are my favourites, mostly because I'm curious
as to what is currently being written and performed, but
also because I admire those people with the audacity to
tell us what they think of someone else's work.

I never read television reviews since they don't seem to serve any purpose. If you watch a new television program then you know whether it's good or bad, and if you didn't see it what possible difference does it make? Movie reviews are likely a good idea, but I personally distrust them since they are usually in the same edition as full-page advertisements that have been purchased to promote the movie. What are the chances of someone saying a movie stinks if you know it is helping to pay your salary? It is like travel writers whose columns praising the exotic tourist attractions of Bali are nestled between expensive ads for the same country.

Probably my admiration for reviewers is based on the fact that I am such a poor one. Over the years, I have been asked to write many book reviews. While I have complied, I have never felt comfortable about it. For me the old axiom "If you can't say something good, don't say anything" seems to apply. In addition, publishers tend to send me books written by people I know, which makes it very difficult to be nasty.

I am sometimes sent pre-publication manuscripts to read so that an excerpt of my remarks can be printed on the book cover. It can be a real challenge to come up with phrases suitably ambiguous. As Groucho Marx once said, "It took me so long to write the review that I never got around to reading the book."

I learned long ago that I was completely hopeless at

theatre criticism. In the early '60s I worked in radio in St. Catharines, Ontario, and as part of my programming duties attended the weekly plays at the Garden Centre Theatre in Vineland. At that time, the highly respected critic Herbert Whittaker wrote for the *Globe and Mail.* Whenever he was unable to make the trip, I was asked by the paper to review the opening-night performance. Dutifully, I would sit through the play, make copious notes, then phone in my comments by 11 p.m., in time for the next morning's edition. One night when Whittaker was on hand, he approached me at intermission.

"You are certainly a very lucky theatre-goer," he said.

"Why is that?" I asked.

He replied, "Because every time you come, it seems to be a terrific performance. Every time I come it's lousy."

The fact of the matter is that I have so much respect and admiration for performers who can walk out on stage, remember their lines and entertain a live audience, I think everything they do is wonderful. My wife claims if actors merely appeared and recited the alphabet I'd give them a standing ovation.

My other failing is my unflagging belief in a proven artist's continued excellence. I can't conceive of Margaret Atwood writing badly. To me, every Alice Munro short story is a jewel and Maureen Forrester never sings off-key.

I should have learned from an experience I had once in London at a special art exhibition featuring an extensive display of Rembrandt paintings. I was filming a television program and my guest was Dr. W.A. Visser 't Hooft. He was, at the time, the first general-secretary of the World Council of Churches but was better known by many as a world authority on the great artist.

He guided me past the paintings, explaining as we went the many intricacies of light and shadow, colour and texture of each masterpiece. When he deliberately ignored one I stopped him and asked, "What about this one?"

"Oh, that is not a very good effort."

"But, how is that possible?" I protested.

"You should always bear in mind," he answered, "even Rembrandt had his bad days."

Sometimes All It Takes Is Encouragement
JULY 1993

Her name was Laura. She was 17 and loved horses.

She told me all this one time while filling my gas tank at the small service station/variety store where she worked. Her age came up when I chided her for not being at school. She said she had finished Grade 12 and wanted to work. Horses became the topic of conversation as she mentioned stopping several times to pet the animals when she rode her bike past our family farm.

"They gallop over to the fence to see me. I especially like the big grey one. Could I possibly ride her some day?"

I told her she was welcome to visit the farm and ride the grey mare whenever she had the time as long as she saw to its grooming, feeding and watering when she was finished. For the next few weeks that summer, I would notice her around the barn or see her enjoying a trot over the pasture fields or through the woods.

One hot July afternoon, as I was absorbed in some writing at the kitchen table, she came in the house for a cool drink of water.

"What are you doing?" she asked.

"I'm writing a book," I replied.

She paused, and slowly said, "Writing a book. Hmmm. You know, I don't think I've actually read a book. A whole one, that is."

I told her I found it hard to believe that anyone could get that far in school and not read a book. How about text-books? How about reading lists? How about book reports?

She explained, "Textbooks don't count. You never read them cover to cover. You can lie about reading lists. Anyone can do book reports from reading the jacket, seeing the movie or cribbing prepared notes."

"But why go to all that bother? Why not just read the book?"

"Nobody I know seems to read much. There are so many other things to do. Also, reading is homework. It's something I have to do as an assigment. I feel as though reading is punishment for something."

My surprise gave way to sadness as I thought of what she had missed in her young life by not discovering the wonderful world of books. I remembered how my parents had encouraged me to read everything possible on the printed page and how, in turn, my children were read to as babies, then provided with the old classics and introduced to new writers as their tastes changed and developed.

"I'll make you a deal," I said. "There's a book in my library called *My Friend Flicka* by Mary O'Hara. It's about a horse. I'd like you to read it before you ride the grey mare again." She agreed.

Two days later she was back, full of excitement about this sentimental story of a boy and his foal. "I hated to put it down. I really wanted it to go on," she said.

"As a matter of fact it does," I told her. I loaned her the sequel, *Thunderhead, Son of Flicka*, and, subsequently, every book I had about horses.

As the summer progressed, I would see her slouched in the saddle, deeply engrossed in a new book as the grey mare wandered about, aimlessly grazing its way from field to field. By September, she was into historical novels and had discovered Agatha Christie mysteries, but I was not to see her again. Her father was given a job transfer and she and her family moved west.

In the new year, I received a card from her. She had enrolled in college and was planning to be a nurse. She had read a biography of Edith Cavell.

This all happened about ten years ago. I get a note from her now and again, usually around midsummer. She is now teaching nursing in an Alberta hospital. She asks about the farm and the family, reminisces about her days as a gas jockey and always includes a long list of books that she thinks I should read.

Losing the Real Meaning of Words in the Fog of Common Usage
NOVEMBER 1995

I have always had a fascination for words. As a child, my parents would never answer me when I asked what a certain word meant, except to say, "Look it up." Our old Thorndike-Barnhart dictionary was a well-thumbed volume. When I began as a newspaper reporter, a very conscientious editor seemed to take delight in blue-pencilling words and phrases in my copy that didn't come up to his standards.

Radio presented a new challenge. Not only did I have to know what the word meant but it had to sound right. All shadings of regional pronunciation must disappear. In the area where I grew up, most people managed to put an "r" in "wash." The capital of the United States became "Warshington." Many stations followed the CBC's rules of pronunciation. That's where I learned not to pronounce the *t* in often; iron sounded just as it looked, not "iern"; Toronto had three distinct syllables, not "Trawna"; the Canadian way to say schedule is "shedule."

I also learned the trick of substitution. One day, a fellow announcer and I were listening to a new commercial. The jingle proclaimed, "Auto*mo*bile, auto*mo*bile, best buy today is Chevrolet." I had always pronounced it *auto*mobile. "Which do you say?" I asked my friend. He answered, "I always say car."

When I was director of programming at a radio station in the '60s, I asked a newly hired announcer why he was not giving coverage to the Vietnam conflict. "Oh, I never read any international news," he said. "I can't pronounce half of the words."

Some people have difficulty getting their tongues around certain words or phrases. I always had trouble with "Progressive Conservative." It had nothing to do with my political leanings; I just found it hard to say. Part of a standard radio audition used to include, "He lived at Rural Route 3, Truro." Applicants who could say that three times distinctly passed.

The University of New Brunswick recently started a course to train professors to speak more intelligibly. Apparently, many students can't understand some of their teachers' speech patterns, pronunciations or accents.

Then there is gobbledygook. Liverpool-born Chrissie Maher has spent her adult life in a quest to persuade people to "call a long-handled, broad-bladed digging instrument a spade." She says that in Britain rambling mumble-speak tends toward endless, revolving sentences in which meaning loses its way. On this side of the Atlantic, tongues are more often tied by the imperative for so-called political correctness. She cites "fiscal underachievers" (poor people), "revenue enhancement" (tax hikes) and "difficult exercises in labour relations" (strikes).

I found when interviewing for television that politicians, the military and social workers had a penchant for gobbledygook. "Involuntary conversion of a 747" (it crashed). "Vertically deployed anti-personnel device" (a bomb). "Wooden interdental stimulation" (a toothpick). "Behaviour-transition corridor" (a school hallway).

I believe some speakers and writers think the use of convoluted phrases makes them sound more intelligent. I was always impressed by Albert Einstein's response when asked if he would briefly explain relativity: "When you are courting a nice girl, an hour seems like a second. When you sit on a red-hot cinder, a second seems like an hour. That's relativity."

Learning Goes Beyond the Three Rs
OCTOBER 1992

If only the joy of reading for its own sake could infuse the entire education system. Many students find their places of learning unbearable prisons where they will serve the required time, emerging with very little learning and much frustration. The fact that some universities feel they have to give literacy tests prior to graduation is an indication of how few students read voraciously.

When asked why we send children to school in the first place the average person will answer, "So they can get a job," or "So they can fit into the workplace." Business leaders and politicians are constantly complaining about the lack of skills that new graduates possess and call for massive funds to be used for retraining in order to save our country's economy. Education to them is the key to commercial success.

Perhaps an education system that has to be tinkered with to meet political goals can't be expected to turn out citizens any wiser than the politicians who manipulated it. School programs that simply pander to the needs of the business community can't be expected to produce workers with any more imagination than the business leaders who define those needs.

In a country that is suffering from a lack of wise politicians and a dearth of conscientious business leaders, we must have an education system whose educators are free to set their own agendas and whose goal is to help their students rise above the muddled minds of our own generation. If all we do is shape students to fit into our society, then surely we have failed. We succed when it is the students who are able to shape a new society. Politicians simply aren't qualified to set that kind of education agenda.

More and more people are calling for a return to the basics. Unfortunately, this is interpreted as a return to the so-called three Rs. The basics of education should be to discover the joy of learning, freeing the mind to explore the means of building a better and more humane world.

Recently, Albert College in Belleville, Ontario, announced the start of a dynamic new teaching approach. It combines the latest in technology with effective teaching methods to "get the students excited about learning." For example, students will be teamed up with Writers in Electronic Residence at Simon Fraser University in B.C. They will electronically submit their writing assignments such as short stories, essays or poems to professional Canadian writers, who will evaluate them, suggest improvements and return them by modem. Another key feature is the cross-curriculum approach to learning. Studies will be integrated, not compartmentalized. Dean of academics at Albert College, Doug Jodoin, explains that students studying science may learn about forces by examining the relative weights a bridge might be able to bear. This would lead perhaps to historical avenues of investigation of famous bridges in history or perhaps to the location of modern bridges. It could be related to art and famous paintings of bridges or to literature such as Michener's *The Bridges at Toko-ri*.

Many new teaching methods have been tried in this country over the years. Many have failed. What I like about this one is that it has been designed by teachers who themselves know the joy of learning and who understand the immense potential of the curious young mind. It is not fashioned for the sole purpose of fitting a person into some niche in the ever-changing and perhaps non-existent job market.

When we stop treating students like cost-effective machines that can be made ever more efficient in order to boost our nation's economy we will have made a huge leap forward in the field of human learning.

One of the saddest comments I heard recently was at a convention where the keynote speaker paraphrased to his business audience, "If you give a man a fish you feed him for a day, but if you teach him to fish you'll see a big jump in sales of fishing gear."

For too long this has been our attitude toward education.

Memo to a Big, Confusing World
MARCH 1996

For a number of years I have been visiting high schools, teaching courses on how to watch television and other media-related subjects. And now teaching journalism at the University of Regina, I meet a lot of young people and listen to their varied concerns.

At the university level, problems tend to centre around relationships with partners or spouses, money for food and tuition fees, uncertainty about the job market and, very often, the future of the planet. These are highly motivated and serious people. They have spent three or four years tuning their intellects and sharpening their skills in a discipline of choice. At this stage in life, problem solving usually just involves discussion, exchanging ideas and pointing out options.

At the high school level, our teenagers are noisy and open about what bugs them. They are teed off with parents, teachers, boyfriends and girlfriends, worried about their appearance and fed up with troublesome siblings. They complain about invasion of privacy and nagging adults. Generally, when they come to see me they just want to let off steam. I tell them that is a good idea but the trick is to do it without screaming, moaning or calling people names.

Recently at a seminar on creative writing, I assigned about 20 Grade 10 and 11 students to write their honest feelings in the form of a memo to their teacher, to the media, to their parents, to our politicians and to themselves. I asked them to hand in their memos the next day. I couldn't possibly reprint all of their comments. What follows is roughly what they wrote.

To my teacher: Get off my back. Don't take it out on me. I know your wages have been frozen. I know your hours have been increased. That's not my fault. My parents pay taxes for me to be here. Just teach me and leave your attitude at home. A word of explanation would be nice now and then. Just handing back a paper with a C-minus doesn't really help me at all.

To the media: I need to laugh but I also would like some information. How come all those families in the sitcoms have such beautiful homes? Nobody I know lives like that. I do not need to see holes in the head spouting blood. I really don't need to see somebody else having sex. Don't talk down to me.

To my parents: Lay off. I'll do my best. When my school evaluation comes back saying that I am not "living up to expectations," I assume it means yours or theirs. How about mine? I know I give you a hard times sometimes. You've got your problems, well, so have I. June Callwood says we will never become mature until we forgive our parents. I forgive you. Do you forgive me?

To our politicians: Don't lie to me. It is not true that everyone in this country thinks the deficit is the first priority of government. It is not true that profit made at the top trickles down to people at the bottom. It is not true that free trade is creating 500,000 new jobs. It is not true that we should copy American social policy.

To myself: I am not a bad person. Perhaps I could try a little harder but I want to do other things too. I want to be liked and thought of as special. I'm in no hurry to grow up. Looking at some older people makes me a little scared of being like them. I would really like to make a difference in the world, I just haven't figured out how to do it yet.

Reading, Writing and Changing the World

MAY 1992

The education gurus are at it again. About once a year, we are informed by poll takers and statisticians that we have dumb kids. This time, the story is that elementary school children in Canada scored lower in math tests than their counterparts in Hungary and Italy.

This gives the education critics their opportunity to say, "We've got to get back to the basics. Back to the three Rs." The culprit is apparently some form of liberalism supposedly introduced to the education system in the '70s. There seems to be a widespread belief that somehow education was better in the distant past.

I often hear people of my generation say, "Boy, when I was in school they taught me how to read and write all right." I think they have short memories. I recall very well, going to high school in the '40s, a lot of people did not learn how to read and write "all right."

Our teachers were hardly out of high school themselves and in many cases shouldn't have been allowed to influence young minds. Teaching by rote and then regurgitating it back through constant exams turned many young people away from the education process. It was hard to discover "the joy of learning." Those of us who had trouble with the basics simply repeated them year after year until we were 16, when we disappeared.

Back then, struggling learners who today are served up a special education menu just ceased to be part of the system. Today we're helping into post-secondary education people who, a generation ago, wouldn't have made it very far into high school.

The present-day rating of our students' knowledge is carried out by university groups funded by businesses with an interest in educational trends. The questions are generally designed to find out how employable our young people are. What are their marketable skills? How are their math and science scores? Are they computer-literate? I think there are more important questions to be asked, answers to which have little or nothing to do with math.

Take a look at the environment. This planet isn't being transformed into an orbiting cesspool because our elementary students haven't memorized their times tables. We are poisoning the world because our political leaders are immobilized by indecision, because industry is propelled by greed and because all of us are selfishly attempting to maintain our comfortable lifestyles while pretending we're not playing a role in the destruction.

Discovering a way to help the starving of the world or prevent war will not depend on algebra grades.

Of all the things we have ever wanted from education, paramount has been the dream of a better society. Education has always been thought of as a defence against so many of the evils that can befall humankind. Education is our best bet to improve the quality of life for all. It will, however, take strong leadership in education to express and promote these aspirations when people with influence are telling us that computer programming is all that's really important.

Some schools still distribute those little pamphlets from the ministry of education that indicate how much you can expect to make in your lifetime if you reach Grade 10 and how much more you can make if you finish Grade 12 or go on to university. This kind of thinking promotes the belief that education is essentially for getting a job and making money.

If education can help students better understand themselves and help them reach out to others, then perhaps they'll be able to change the world *and* hold down that steady job. But if they can only manage one, I'd prefer they change the world.

Heading West to a Whole New Life
SEPTEMBER 1995

It's been quite a few years since I've held down a regular job. The majority of people I meet tend to greet me with the question, "How are you enjoying your retirement?" I never know how to respond.

I stopped being the host of CBC's *Man Alive* program in 1989. This suggested to many Canadians that I went back to the farm, put my feet up and began collecting a pension. Not so. Despite the fact that being involved in a major weekly documentary production was a full-time, often hectic, always fulfilling assignment, I suddenly found I was busier than I had been in the preceding 22 years.

Speaking engagements, writing commitments and broadcasting opportunities that I had been unable to accept because of contract restrictions came rolling in. New projects and proposals were suggested. Memberships on boards dealing with government, education and charitable fundraising were offered. Publishers wanted books. Magazines wanted articles. Corporations wanted commercial endorsements. Agencies wanted seminars. It became a problem not of finding something to do but of finding time in which to do what I wanted.

Clearly I would have to set up some kind of criteria for my work choices. My wife, children and grandchildren joined in helping sort out priorities. I felt their love, support and encouragement.

It was decided I would only give the speeches, write the articles, join the boards and support the causes where I truly felt I could do the most good. My family taught me that saying no was not a bad thing. I would include time for my own personal nourishment by pursuing hobbies that I enjoyed: gardening, cooking, reading, attending plays and concerts. Perhaps I would even fulfil a lifelong ambition and learn how to play the banjo.

I discovered the happy balance of a public and personal lifestyle.

I rationed my time. If I had been in Halifax for a convention on Wednesday, I'd spend Thursday on the farm chopping wood. If Friday found me with politicians in Ottawa, the weekend would see me with grandchildren at home.

Then came 1995. A year of surprises. Another honorary degree, a college diploma, appointment as honorary colonel in the Canadian Armed Forces, the proud but humbling experience of receiving the Order of Canada. And, as of September, a whole career change. I accepted the position of professor of journalism at the University of Regina.

The position is called the Max Bell Chair. George Maxwell Bell was born in Regina in 1912. Starting with the *Calgary Albertan*, he built a newspaper empire that included the *Winnipeg Free Press*, *Ottawa Journal*, *Victoria Times-Colonist*, *Montreal Star*, and the *Globe and Mail*, to name a few. By the mid-'60s, more Canadians read his newspapers than any other. He was an avid sportsman with investments in hockey and racehorses. In 1965 his horse Meadow Court won the Irish Derby; another won the Queen's Plate. He was a vigorous, affable and deeply religious man. A journalism chair named in his honour is a fitting tribute to this great Canadian.

I've never been a professor before. As a matter of fact, I've never been to university. But don't tell the folks in Regina that.

They think they're rescuing me from retirement.

Obscuring the Glow of Excellence

FEBRUARY 1996

When I started teaching last September at the School of Journalism, University of Regina, I knew it would take a while to get up to speed with the new technology. Although I am still regularly involved in newspaper, radio, magazine and TV, there have been remarkable changes since I toiled for a living in these media vineyards.

Editing of tape and film is now done electronically, not with scissors and sticky patches. Research is accomplished at the touch of a computer key, not by rummaging through dusty files or microfiche. The old noisy, cluttered ambience of the newsroom that I knew has been replaced by a quietly humming efficiency. Editors and proofreaders are becoming extinct, victims of spell-check software. (Not always with good results. A recent front-page editorial in the local paper proclaimed "Pope Seeks Piece.")

Now well into the second semester, I think I've finally got the hang of it. There are other professors who are light years ahead of me technically, so I concentrate on product and content. I am still wrestling, however, with one concern that has emerged.

Near the end of last year I received a call from my friend Pierre Berton, who said he would be in town the next day. I asked him if he would mind meeting with my students and he agreed with alacrity. Things went well as Pierre exhorted, cajoled and lectured the students in his inimitable style, drawing on his vast experience in practically every branch of communications. When it came time for questions I noticed considerable reticence on the part of the students to speak up. Later, some came to my office and apologized. "You see, Roy, we would have gotten more involved but we didn't know who he was." It was clear they have never read his newspaper columns or magazine articles, watched *The Pierre Berton Show* or *Front Page Challenge*. "But the man has written 39 books," I protested. "Surely you must have stumbled over one of them or watched the televised version."

"Sorry, no," was the reply.

My classes were to be devoted to seminars. Would it do any good to arrange for a visit by W.O. Mitchell or Farley Mowat? Would I be wasting my time to secure June Callwood or Peter Newman? If recognition depends on your face being seen on the tube daily or your name constantly in the headlines, does this just leave me with David Letterman or Oprah Winfrey? I wonder if some people got to know Robertson Davies only through his obituary tributes or televised funeral.

At the beginning of my career, or any time during, I would have jumped at the chance to have a chat with Edward R. Murrow or Stephen Leacock. Could it be there are some people entering the field of science today who would look blank if introduced to Stephen Hawking or Roberta Bondar?

Certainly one of my seminars will centre on the media's ability to obscure proven excellence with flashy mediocrity. I am not singling out students with this concern. Recently at a house party I was mourning the loss of another friend, Bruno Gerussi. "Oh, yes," a guest remarked, "he had a very good cooking show." Here was the man described by Sir Laurence Olivier as the greatest Romeo in the history of Shakespearean theatre being remembered for his lasagne recipe.

I Learned a Lot of Things
SEPTEMBER 1996

One of the more delightful experiences I had during my visiting professorship last semester was a few sessions spent teaching at the Seniors' Education Centre. The centre is part of the university's extension program and provides education, stimulation and social interaction to older members of the community. I was told by director John Oussoren to expect 30 to 40 students in attendance. Over 100 showed up in one of the coldest, inhospitable winters Regina had seen in 30 years. Ages varied. In one session, I described the categories that were generally used to indicate stages of aging: 55 to 65 — the Young Old; 65 to 75 — the Old; 75 to 90 — the Old-Old. Immediately one woman raised her hand and exclaimed, "Don't leave me out." She was 95.

With outside temperatures hovering around –40 Celsius and the prairie wind taking it even lower with the chill factor, we basked in the warmth of friendship, shared discussion and rollicking good humour.

There's a palpable difference between teaching the old and the young. First of all there is not really much new information you can impart to an 80-year-old. To use a currently popular expression, they've "been there, done that." They are not reticent in giving their opinions, never shy in challenging your views, often managing to reverse the roles of instructor and learner. The atmosphere is certainly more relaxed. There is not the youth-laden pressure of assignment deadlines, tuition fees or parental expectations.

I'm sure they found my teaching efforts amusing. My lecture "Society's Treatment of the Elderly" was obviously redundant. My presentation "The History of Broadcasting" must have sounded like a rerun. Our most successful sessions turned out to be "The Telling of Stories." I read from my book, *There Was a Time . . .* , some of the tales of growing up as a farm boy in Eastern Ontario. My only assignment was for them to "go forth and do likewise." My, did they respond.

A flood of anecdotes, vignettes, short stories, poems and mood pieces landed on my desk. They obviously didn't need a course in creative writing. I read several of their efforts aloud in class and the seed of an idea was born. Why not collect the best of these stories and publish them in a book? Director Oussoren headed the project and turned the editing responsibilities over to two students with editorial experience, Jockie-Loomer Kruger and her husband, Herb. Within weeks, the manuscript was at the printers complete with old photographs to illustrate the material. Then, someone suggested I record the stories on audio cassette that could accompany the book for a complete reading and listening package. Of course, I agreed.

I had told them the story of my great-aunt Et, who had come to live with our family of 12 when she was 90 years old. For six wonderful years she passed on her life experiences to me. I used to chide her when, at the end of some wonderful tale, she would say, "Oh my, ya shoulda' been there," not realizing that the event was likely 50 or so years before I was born. When I would remind her of this she would pause, look somewhat bewildered, then say, "Well, ya shoulda' been there anyway!" The Seniors' Group honoured that story by calling their book, and the cassette, *Ya Shoulda' Been There*.

The importance of passing on living history from one generation to the next cannot be overly stressed. I would like to see our elders from coast to coast write down and record the moments of their lives that have lingered in their memories. When I read Hattie Pawson's recollection of the Regina Riot of 1935, or Eleanor Chance Long's poem about an old steam engine called the *Prairie Express*, or Trevor Quinn's description of early radio and Saturday-night baths, I feel I've been given a piece of Canada. I'm glad these treasures did not slip away.

If any seniors' group would like to embark on a similar venture, I'm sure Jockie and Herb would be happy to explain what is involved to make it a success. They could be reached through the Seniors' Education Centre, University of Regina, S4S 0A2. Incidentally, if you'd like your own copy, *Ya Shoulda' Been There* can be ordered by sending a $20 cheque to the Seniors' Centre. All proceeds go to the Centre.

What's Your Sign?
NOVEMBER 1996

I have always been a sign reader. It is probably not a good idea these days to take your eyes off the road, but I find it hard to resist a well-worded message on post, wall, bumper or billboard. Let me hasten to add, however, that I do not care for the slick, unrelenting barrage of high-tech advertising that lines our streets and freeways. I prefer the simple straight-to-the-point signs that say what they mean clearly and concisely. If they show a sense of humour, so much the better.

I remember an old real-estate sign on the lawn of a house for sale that said "If you lived here, you'd be home now." The bumper sticker that proclaimed "If you can read this, you are too close" has recently been changed to

"If you can read this, thank a teacher." This shows imagination and has a definite meaning. For years, on Jarvis Street in Toronto, a small sandwich-board outside of a hardware store has had only three simple words, Good Paint Cheap. What more is there to say? I remember many years ago on a visit to Timmins, Ontario, seeing a cardboard notice in a store window that, if more delicately phrased, would have said Manure for Sale. In Belleville, Ontario, there is a one-block street with a sign that reads University Avenue South. A glance down the road will quickly show that it has no university on it, neither does it have a north. Driving in Saskatchewan last year I came to a stop on a remote highway at a pictorial deer-crossing sign. There were ten deer proudly crossing the road at the precise spot indicated. I could imagine them conferring earlier and deciding the safest spot to cross was obviously at the sign.

Travel presents wonderful opportunities to see new signs. Pictures replace words to warn of falling rock in B.C.'s interior, elephants crossing in India, kangaroos and emus in Australia, musk ox in Norway.

On my first visit to Rome, I marvelled at how the city was so well posted with directions to the Spanish Steps, Piazza Navona, Trevi Fountain, the Coliseum, and other attractions. I kept trying to find the place that several signs pointed to called Senso Unico. Finally, after asking directions, I found out it meant one way street.

Attempts to translate signs into English are often

humorous. On the back of a hotel room door in Venice
was a notice warning me I would be "punished if under-
wear was washed in the sink." In his book *A Year in
Provence*, Peter Mayle tells of a neighbour who found his
Beware of Dog sign did not deter trespassers. He solved
the problem by changing it to Beware of Vipers.

Cemeteries are interesting places to find succinct notices.
A visit to the Boothill graveyard in Tombstone, Arizona,
shows many examples of how a big event can be con-
densed. One marker says "John Heath, Lynched by Bisbee
Mob." Another states "George Johnston, Hanged by Mistake."
Then there is the doggerel epitaph to Lester Moore:

> Here lies Lester Moore,
>
> Four shots from a .44
>
> No Les, no more.

Since most of the grave markers are testimony to murder, hanging, shooting and killing, it is almost startling to
see one that says "M.E. Kellogg, Died a Natural Death."

The more convoluted signage likely began with the old
Burma-Shave signs that were arranged sequentially along
American Highways during the '40s and '50s. They came
down in the '60s when the company was sold to a razor
manufacturer:

> Around the curve,
>
> Lickety-split,
>
> It's a beautiful car,
>
> Wasn't it! — Burma-Shave.

They were amusing, usually carried a safety message and, I'm sure, sold a lot of shaving cream. Today our billboards flicker and change with several strident slogans grabbing for our attention at once. Our skyline is punctured with golden arches, giant balloons and plastic buckets of chicken.

Somehow, the simple hand-painted sign by the side of the road that said "Eats" said it all.

8

FEELING THE SPIRIT

"Every time I
Feel the spirit
Moving in my heart
I will pray."

— OLD SPIRITUAL

There Are As Many Kinds of Prayer As There Are People Praying

JUNE 1995

Part of the power of prayer is its ability to bring people together in a shared response. I experienced some of that power after writing an article about prayer that prompted readers to share their personal feelings and experiences on the subject.

Murray Garnett tells of being a Sunday school teacher in Downsview, Ontario, when, during a lesson on prayer, a young boy asked permission to give a demonstration. The lad distorted his left hand into the palm of his erect right hand and prayed, "Please, God, make my one hand like the other one." His right hand suddenly convulsed into a gnarled position. Murray says the whole class, including the teacher, got the point.

In a wonderful story about a boy whose prayer experiences finally result in a bicycle, John Grieve concludes with this summary. "Is all asking right? I doubt it if one demands, or barters, 'God, I'll do so and so forever if you'll only do this for me now.' We are all interconnected, our wants and needs overlap and sometimes conflict with one another. When we ask together we remove some of the conflict and can sort out some of the consequences but we cannot possibly foresee all the ramifications of getting what we are asking for."

Another correspondent (who did not want to be identified) writes: "Prayer and dogma have little in common. One can pray very well without believing in the immaculate conception or without knowing what is inside the 'blue book' of the United Church. Sometimes you have a feeling God is not listening today. Don't worry. Try again tomorrow. Think about accepting the things you cannot change and changing the things you can."

Ed Barks suggests, "If you would talk with God in prayer you must know humility and live humility. Without this you will be talking to yourself in prayer, rather than with God. If, with a humble heart, you take a problem to God in prayer each question will be answered with a question until the response is either, 'You now have the problem properly defined, Go into the world, Seek and ye shall find the answer,' or 'Go in peace, you have given us the answer to your problem.' "

One more personal reminiscence. In the fall of 1976, just before the U.S. general election, I did a television program about candidate Jimmy Carter. I went to Plains, Georgia, and talked with neighbours and relatives of Carter to find out what kind of a person this born-again peanut farmer was. At the recently held Democratic National Convention, Carter had been highly praised in a speech by Martin Luther King Sr. Our television crew stopped off in Atlanta so I could interview the venerable old Baptist preacher and father of the great civil rights leader.

In the hot Georgia sun, seated near the simple but beautiful memorial to his martyred son, King was the picture of Christian benevolence and charity until we got on the subject of prayer.

"Do you pray for Jimmy Carter?" I asked.

"Oh yes, daily."

"Do you pray for Gerald Ford?"

"I pray for most everybody, but I ain't going to ask God to bless Gerald Ford."

"Why not? He's the president," I insisted.

"I ain't going to ask God's blessing on a man so's he can keep on doing the wrong thing," was his reply.

Like Beauty, the Power of Prayer Is in the Eye of the Beholder
FEBRUARY 1995

Prayers can be such a personal thing, and when invited the first time to someone's home for dinner I've often experienced that awkward pause before the meal begins. Do they or do they not say grace? Until I hear "dig in" or "let us return thanks," I just sit silently contemplating my soup.

At a dinner party over the Christmas holidays our host did say a short blessing, which prompted one of the guests, perhaps emboldened by his pre-dinner aperitif, to ask the rationale for prayer at mealtime or any other occasion. "Do we really think God is actually listening to our petitions or are we just doing it to make ourselves feel good?" This prompted a lively and interesting discussion of prayer in general — a topic I have always found fascinating. Our host admitted that he said grace mostly out of habit but that he truly was grateful for the food and company and just wanted to go on record as saying so. Another guest told of surviving a serious illness recently and was convinced that it was the intercessions of her friends and loved ones that pulled her through. This encouraged others to join in with their views, some openly sceptical of the value of trying to talk to God, others fervent in their belief in the power of prayer.

Over the years, interviewing people for television or radio, I have often tacked on an extra question or two about prayer regardless of the subject under discussion. I'm sure this was partly due to my own confusion but also because the replies were so revealing. For your consideration, here are some of the answers I recorded.

Jean Vanier: "I believe that when we enter into the world of prayer God sends his spirit. The spirit of God teaches us to love and you can't enter into the world of love without loving your brothers and your sisters. It's an opening up to other people — to their suffering, their joys, their peace. And this opening up of our beings is the world of prayer. Prayer can be a kind of therapy that brings equilibrium, peace, strength and internal force. One must not forget, however, that prayer is essentially adoration and thanksgiving."

Chief Dan George: "When I pray I say to God, 'Make me wise so that I may know the things that you have taught your children, the lessons you have hidden in every leaf and rock. Make me strong, not to be superior to my brothers, but to be able to fight my greatest enemy — myself. Make me ever ready to come to you with straight eyes, so that when my life fades, as the fading sunset, my spirit will come to you without shame.' "

David Steindl-Rast, Benedictine monk and student of Zen: "Prayer is gratitude. Living life gratefully is not taking things for granted. When you take things for granted you go through life where nothing is meaningful to you. You should stop and consider the given reality even though it may not always be the kind of gift that you really want — it's a gift, and the only appropriate response to a gift is 'thank you.' If we cultivate those moments in our daily life when we are filled with gratefulness and those times when we can act gratefully, then we are putting prayer on a kind of human level, which in many ways is a much deeper religious context."

Just as prayer can be a highly personal thing, so can that age-old record of a family's prayers, the family Bible.

Family History Between the Pages
FEBRUARY 1993

I treasure my immense undated edition of the Holy Bible, which proclaims on the frontispiece, "with Apocrypha, Psalms in Metre and Marginal References and Readings, plus Brown's Concordance to the Holy Scriptures, to which are added, A Pictorial History of the Books of the Bible, with Several Hundred Engravings on Wood and Steel." It weighs about ten pounds and is not something you grab for quick reference or to read in bed.

It has become a treasure chest of family memorabilia recalling moments in the lives of my ancestors for many generations. Between the Old and New Testaments are six pages in gold, red and purple hues that list marriages, births and deaths. They are all full. The earliest entry is 1871 and the latest is 1976.

Scattered throughout its pages is a veritable history of relatives and friends who touched and departed, leaving this trail of remembrance. Yellowed newspaper clippings testify to happy events such as school graduations, elections to community organizations and honeymoon travels. There are a lot of black-bordered cards that begin with the words "Laid to Rest."

There are receipts from church donations and Sunday school givings and a couple of envelopes from the 1800s that apparently were never handed in that read "For our Worn Out Ministers."

There are many colourful maple, oak and hickory leaves, now crisp and fragile, along with a few roses pressed flat and brown, and corsages that still speak of romantic encounters. Locks of hair are discovered throughout its pages, mostly unidentified. One blond curl wrapped in tissue paper is labelled "Roy." Four-leafed clovers, snatches of poetry, pieces of ribbon abound.

I think it was originally owned by my grandmother's sister. Her marriage certificate is preserved in Genesis. From then on, we can only guess who decided what was important enough to be so enshrined.

Was this a custom that only happened in bygone years before the invention of the filing cabinet? Does anyone save things in a Bible any more? A quick check of my other old books fails to reveal anything hidden between the pages. Some people likely keep bits of nostalgia in boxes, dresser drawers or scrapbooks, but I suspect the majority of us just toss them out. A cynic might say that these items were put in the big family Bible because there would be little risk of them being disturbed.

I like to think it was done so that they could be looked at and admired on a more regular basis.

Family Bible Sorted and Filed Our Lives
MAY 1994

Not long after writing about my old family bible and some of the items that had been stored between its pages, I received a letter from Rev. Robert Thaler, who serves the New Hamburg Pastoral Charge in Ontario. He says, "I think people saved things in their family Bible because God and the stories of the Bible were the patterns by which they found meaning for what happened in their own lives. A photo, a clipping or a recipe stuck between the pages placed some specific event or person in the context of God. In this framework it made sense."

A most interesting theory. According to Thaler the Bible was not used as a scrapbook, a filing cabinet or a simple repository for memorabilia, but as a vehicle to make a certain statement about special family events or treasures.

From a sermon he once delivered at a Flower Service while in Victoria-Freshwater, Newfoundland, comes this story:

"A long time ago, I got a call that a Mrs. Brown, aged over 80, had died and would I come over to her house. When I arrived the undertakers had already taken Mrs. Brown away and her daughter and two sons were sitting at the kitchen table. They invited me in and we sat down to a cup of tea to talk about their mother, their grief and their plans. There on the kitchen table was Mrs. Brown's Bible. It had been well handled, much of the blacking had worn off and the brown leather showed through. Sometimes, when you are a minister you don't know the people that you have to bury too well, so you listen to the family and friends to get to know the person.

"I opened the cover of the Bible and between the pages were all sorts of slips of paper and newspaper clippings and old photographs. It seemed that I had stumbled on the one cluttered corner of Mrs. Brown's life. She had kept a spotless house and immaculate gardens, and as I wandered through the pages, looked at the photos and read the slips of paper, it became clear that the clutter was in fact organized.

"The photographs weren't in any chronological order but seemed to be placed in special spots and so were the clippings and the scraps of poetry and letters. On the thin white pages of the Bible itself there wasn't a mark but here and there were bits of paper with Scripture verses written out in full."

Thaler goes on to describe pictures of "Grandma Smith, Mom and me," dated 1912 and stuck between the pages at Proverbs 31, the passage about a woman of noble character. Another picture of a smiling young man in uniform was placed at the 121st Psalm, the one usually read at Remembrance Day. Mrs. Brown's daughter explained, "That's Uncle Roy, Mom's brother. He was killed in the war, somewhere in France, I think." A picture and note about the death of "Danny, 1925, 5 months and 21 days" is at the passage from Mark where Jesus tells the disciples to let the children come to him.

"So it was all through her Bible," writes Mr. Thaler. "Recipes for spice cooking stuck among the Christmas stories. Arthur's obituary at Psalm 23. A picture of a family reunion with great-grandmother at the centre placed alongside the passage telling us to make a joyful noise. Leah Brown had gathered her life together and laid it along side of the Word of God."

I was delighted to hear this story and of course once

again took down our old family Bible for a closer look. Alas, the Bonisteels weren't the least bit organized. Nothing seemed to match. Although a rather shoddy school report card of my older brother is right beside Ecclesiastes 12:12, "Of making many books there is no end; and much study is a weariness of the flesh."

Stories from Religion's Far Side
APRIL 1993

Certainly, anyone who thinks people of faith are dull or boring hasn't been keeping up with the news.

A group of cultists waving streamers and placards with biblical passages was arrested in Manila recently for slashing car tires and letting the air out. The mass deflating appeared to be well planned, began during rush hour and created huge traffic jams. The leader explained, "This is God's will. Air is from God and this is God's way of stopping bad deeds."

Meanwhile, a different kind of deflating was going on in Binghampton, New York, where a local church announced a Workshop in Lenten Living. Objective? "To shed unwanted pounds and develop new attitudes and eating habits." Lunches were "low in calories but enriched with spiritual advice."

A church in southern Tennessee planned to release 1,000 helium balloons containing cards printed with "Christ

Is Risen." Some of the balloons also contained gift certifi-
cates ranging from 50 cents to $50. "The certificates must
be presented at church school services Easter Sunday to
be redeemed." This sounds like a rather tacky way to boost
attendance, but the pastor explained, "This is to get people of all faiths or no faith involved in the Easter story.
What's wrong with using modern advertising methods to
bring people to God?"

The big news, however, is how religion is taking advantage of our new technology. At a trade fair for religious
items and furnishings in Vicenza, Italy, confessional booths
were unveiled featuring sound-proofing, air conditioning
and comfortable armchairs. One church official in criti-
cizing the idea said the fair's organizers had "turned the
confessional into a space-age telephone booth." Whether
these new, modern conveniences will encourage sinners
to come clean or just enjoy a relaxing visit with the priest
has yet to be determined.

Actually, one may not have to go to church to acknowledge sins any more. It is being proposed that people should
be able to send in their confessions by fax machine. This
high-tech approach to get God's attention has already been
set up in Jerusalem.

For centuries Jews have been making pilgrimages to
the Western or Wailing Wall in that city, many travelling
thousands of miles at great expense for the experience. It
is a common custom to write prayers on little slips of

paper, known in Yiddish as *kvittlach*, that are then poked between the cracks in the wall. It is felt that this will speed their petitions to God. Now, the Israeli telephone company, Bezak, has installed a special line on which you can fax your messages. You can call from anywhere in the world and there is no extra charge to have your fax put in the cracks.

While this sounds a bit strange, it doesn't seem to bother the rabbinical community. Rabbi David Lincoln of the conservative Park Avenue Synagogue in New York says his only fear is that the fax sheets may be too big to fit in the wall and could pose a litter problem. But he adds, "Judaism has always believed in using modern methods so I'm not really scandalized by it. I can't see anything in Jewish law to forbid it."

The only concern came from an executive of the Fax Information Network of America, who pointed out that fax pirates could tap into the messages on the telephone line and tamper with a private communication with God. He pointed out, however, that new technology is on the horizon whereby data can be compressed into a code. "We're developing new ways now to secure messages," he said. "We call it safe fax."

Even if slashing tires, promotional stunts or electronic praying don't fit in with our idea of devotional pursuits, we have to admit that modern religion is not stagnant.

While religion is not stagnant, it is outgrowing many
of the buildings that housed it in the past. This became
apparent to me after a recent phone call.

Hope, Restoration and a Lot of Red Tape
AUGUST 1992

"Would you be interested in doing something with that old church up on the hill?" It was a local United Church minister calling to investigate the possibility of rescuing what had gone from a beloved local landmark to a crumbling shell of brick and plaster. My initial reaction was, "What on earth would I do with that abandoned old eyesore?" That question still hasn't been answered after three years.

The church was built in the square, one-room design with small loft and towering steeple so common to the rural Protestant churches scattered throughout Ontario. Etched in concrete above the entry is "Zion M.E. Church A.D. 1876." It sits high on the hill across the road from my farm and was the structure that always came to mind when, as a child, my mother would take my hands, lace my fingers together, thumbs in front and say, "This is the church, and this is the steeple, open the doors and see all the people." Along with the little brick schoolhouse and local cheese factory, it was the focal point for the entire area. It was where people came together. It was the community.

When church closures began in the '60s, some of these buildings were snapped up by entrepreneurs and turned into commercial enterprises. One in our area became a gas station and truck stop. Another became an apple storage warehouse. Ours closed in 1971. I was asked to give the sermon at the final anniversary service. It was subsequently sold for two dollars to the local Women's Institute and for a few years was a community centre for meetings and wedding receptions and a polling place at election time. Gradually, it became too much to maintain and when the institute branch folded, the front door was nailed shut, the windows were boarded up and it was left to the elements and vandals.

It became a favourite weekend hang-out for town rowdies and local lovers. They pried open the doors, smashed the remaining pews and chairs, stole the stained glass and ripped out the fixtures. Monday mornings would find the surrounding grassy lot strewn with empty beer bottles and used condoms.

Despite not knowing what to do with the church, my wife, Jane, and I decided to rescue it. We couldn't bear to watch the rain sweep in through the roof or the chunks of brick dislodge and tumble from the tower. It did not deserve this desecration. The moment we agreed to buy it, the bureaucratic nightmare began.

The United Church Presbytery, which thought they owned it because of a clause in its contract with the

Women's Institute, didn't. When a non-profit organization folds in this province, all assets revert to the provincial government. In order to retrieve it, a private member's bill had to be passed, and the Women's Institute had to be reconstituted temporarily in order to turn the property back to the presbytery, which in turn could then sell it to us. At this point, lawyers entered the picture. New survey maps were required. An old road allowance that ran through the property was discovered and township approval had to be obtained to have it closed. This required agreement from the owners of all adjacent property. What started out as a simple transference of an old deteriorating building became a three-year morass of paperwork, government red tape, official legalese and frustration. The "mills of the Gods" may grind exceedingly slow but they can't hold a candle to elected officialdom.

However, in what may turn out to be more blind faith than good sense, we have had a new roof installed with thick cedar shingles to match the original. The crumbling brick tower has been entirely replaced and a sturdy fence erected to keep out marauders. I think a little of its former pride is returning.

"What are you going to do with the old church?" is a question Jane and I hear daily. The answer is, we don't know. But this historic landmark will be preserved. This symbol of community inspiration will remain. When you enter the old structure that has meant so much to generations of families, or when you climb the partially finished tower and look out over the countryside, there's a feeling of comfort and stability, a feeling of belonging and hope, a feeling of peace. These are good feelings.

Virtues To Remember in a Time of Change
JUNE 1990

Over the years, because of my association with religious broadcasting, I've often been asked if I grew up in a church family. The answer is yes and no. My mother was involved in the local United Church, my father wasn't. Some of my brothers and sisters were, some weren't. We were a farm family of 12 scraping by as best we could, and I suspect our individual attendance at Sunday services depended on which one had access to the clean shirt.

In an old farm account book of my father's I see sprinkled among the notations of grain sales and cattle breeding dates the information, "Minister here today — gave him $2.00."

My earliest memories of church were of being taken to services on special days like Easter, Christmas, Mother's Day and Temperance Sunday. I especially liked Temperance Sunday because after you filled out the little card swearing never to touch demon alcohol as long as you lived, you were allowed to keep the pencil. But more importantly, I remember it as a happy place where people seemed glad to see you. It didn't matter if you came from the rural area or from town, whether your Sunday clothes were new or patched or when the offering plate was passed you only had a nickel to give — you still got a big smile. You were accepted.

It must have been a tough time for a local church to survive and serve the community, especially with families like ours who only showed up on a hit-and-miss basis. Yet it never held back on extending its warmth and friendship to all.

I have often heard the United Church criticized for being too open, too indiscriminate. "You can't get married in your church? Don't worry, the United Church will marry anybody. You want your baby baptized, your grandmother buried, your teenager straightened out? Call the United Church, they have no restrictions." Some have seen this as a failing. I've always thought of it as a strength.

This feeling of acceptance came again in my mid-twenties when, in a new job in a strange city, I knew where to go to feel welcome. I became heavily involved in youth work in the Hi-C movement and even today bump into people who were teenage members of various groups I led who tell me how much it meant to have been a part of the church at that time in their lives. Later, I was employed by the church in various broadcasting endeavours and was encouraged to share facilities and resources with all denominations and faiths.

I found myself working with United Church people who represented a faith that had no denominational bounds, people who excited and inspired me by their willingness to accept alternative points of view, different lifestyles and varying backgrounds. When I think of the United Church at its best I think of people like Ray Hord, Al Forrest, Lois Boast, Jack Shaver, Ivan Cumming, Keith Woollard and so many like them who did not always do the popular or the safe thing but what they thought to be the right thing.

No organization can remain static and hope to survive. It must change and adapt to reflect the age in which it lives. It should hold fast to the attributes that have sustained it for so long, and surely the United Church would find the virtue of "acceptance" near the top of the list.

Part of the philosophy of acceptance has always been expressed for me in the concept of "moderation in all things," including a little drink now and then.

Mixing Alcohol with a Little Common Sense
MARCH 1992

I enjoy a glass of wine with dinner. I appreciate an icy-cold bottle of beer on a hot hay-making day. I've been known to savour a snifter of fine brandy in front of a cozy fireplace. And I manage to enjoy all this without any trace of guilt.

This was not always the case. My mother never allowed alcoholic beverages in the house. That didn't mean there wasn't drinking going on. It just meant that the "menfolk" hid their cases of beer or jugs of hard cider out behind the barn. Whenever I heard my father suggest to a visiting neighbour that he might like to see a newborn heifer or inspect the alfalfa crop, I knew they would soon be enjoying a clandestine snort or two.

This hypocrisy had a lot to do with our church teaching at the time. Our rural United Church minister preached against the evils of strong drink frequently, and once a year, on Temperance Sunday, everyone over 12 years old was instructed to fill out a pledge card promising to never touch the stuff.

Over the years, I learned that it was not a sin to drink but it was certainly wrong to drink to excess. As a newspaper and radio reporter I covered enough court cases of homicide, drunken driving, assault and battery and family violence to know the incredible damage that can be done while under the influence of alcohol. I saw friends and colleagues ruin their careers and their lives with a seemingly uncontrollable craving for booze. Later, I did television documentaries on the rescue efforts of Alcoholics Anonymous and various addiction centres. I learned that for some complete abstention was the only means of survival. I also saw many people over-indulge at certain times. While they may not have had drinking problems, they did things and acted in ways they would never have considered when sober.

I think we are now seeing a trend to a more sensible approach to alcohol. While there are still far too many drinking drivers, the number has certainly been reduced. Part of this is due to more severe penalties, but I believe the majority of drinkers today are adopting a more responsible attitude. It has been a long time since I was at a party where there were not the requisite number of designated drivers.

Overall consumption of beer, wine and liquor is down nationally. Drinkers are opting for lighter or non-alcoholic beverages or at least fewer trips to the trough. We are discovering the truth in the phrase "you don't have to drink to have a good time." We are appreciating a clearheaded morning-after, complete with the knowledge that we didn't make asses of ourselves.

The church too has become less vitriolic in its condemnation of "demon rum." Many United Church laypersons and ministers alike now share a potent sip without feeling guilty about some transgression.

The first United Church moderator I knew personally was the controversial James. R. Mutchmor. He was known across this country as a most flamboyant and dedicated battler against the evils of alcohol. Yet, in all the interviews I did with him or in the many presentations I heard him give, he never once condemned the drinker. He took on the companies that manufactured strong drink. He fought with governments against their liquor policies. He clashed with agencies that advertised the product, but he was also responsible for the General Council statement of 1960 that said, "A United Church member who abstains from beverage alcohol and one who conscientiously uses it in a reasonable way, are both recognized in good standing."

I hope I am right when I say we are taking a more common-sense approach to drinking. While we must be aware of the ravages caused by over-indulgence, I don't think our pleasures in life should be guilty ones.

Cheers!

Early Signs of Spiritual Renewal
APRIL 1992

For the last 20 years, perhaps more, it seems we've heard nothing but gloomy statistics about religion — dropping enrolment, withering resources, lack of commitment. These have been blamed on everything from the secularization of society to the death of God. Perhaps now we are seeing a turnaround.

Why is there an increased interest in becoming ordained to a career in the church? There could be all kinds of reasons. Perhaps in our more sterile technological world some women and men feel drawn to a profession that is people-oriented. Maybe in a recession, with the resulting lack of jobs, a career as a minister seems secure, relatively well paid and not subject to layoffs. It could be that bludgeoned with daily media reports of violence, hate and tragedy, there are those who feel a genuine calling to serve in some humanitarian way to make this a gentler, more loving world.

At Queen's Theological College in Kingston, principal Clifford Hospital says the increase in students means that the lean years caused by the difficulties the United Church has faced in the past decade are over. The college has had to launch a $500,000 campaign to help finance not only the ministerial studies but also a demand for correspondence courses in theology and scholarships for Third World students.

It may be too early to tell, but there seems to be some kind of North American spiritual revival. Recently in Montreal, I met with several observers of the religious scene to chat about the state of religion in both the United States and Canada.

R. Emmett Tyrrell Jr. is founder and editor-in-chief of the *American Spectator*. He has close links with the more conservative elements of American Christianity. Contrary to popular opinion, he said the scandals that brought down some prominent TV evangelists have not hurt the movement to any significant degree. The Fundamentalist churches are alive and well and gaining new converts every day. He thought society had become too loose and without direction, leaving people with a desire for the structures of a religious faith.

Adam Clayton Powell III, former head of news and information programming for National Public Radio in the United States, said he has noticed many more young people getting involved in their local congregations. "New parents are coming back to the church and are anxious to have their children experience the religious community," he claimed.

Elizabeth Brown, a correspondent for the *Christian Science Monitor*, felt that people were reaching out for something more meaningful than what they were finding in their day-to-day experiences. She too reported a renewed interest in the study of theology.

I also had an opportunity to talk with Heather Thompson. She is chaplain at Bishop's University in Lennoxville, Quebec. I asked her why she thought there was an increase in people who wanted to go into the ministry. She said those entering theological colleges are not the young people we used to see, but men and women in their thirties and forties. "This very often is a second career," she said. "They have been out in the workforce, some are raising a family, and they have found a genuine calling, based on their secular experience, to involve themselves in religious work."

I don't think it really matters whether people are opting to get involved in the church or study theology for fun, profit, curiosity or lifelong commitment. They are entering a fascinating field and I say more power to them.

9

ONCE UPON A CHRISTMAS

The rising of the sun
And the running of the deer,
The playing of the merry organ,
Sweet singing in the choir.

— OLD CAROL

Taking the Rush Out of Christmas
JANUARY 1990

Even before it arrives, some people are tired of Christmas. It's too commercial, they say, or it starts too early and it lasts too long. This time of year when you hear people exclaim "I'll be glad when it's over," you know exactly what they are talking about.

It's true that, for some, the Christmas season has become a big end-of-the-year sale that begins the day after Hallowe'en and ends with half-priced greeting cards on Boxing Day. But that's the Christmas of frantic shopping, competitive decorating and obligatory entertaining. Of all times in our complex lives, Christmas should be anticipated with pleasure, savoured and enjoyed when it's here, remaining gentle on our minds for months after.

The idea of Christmas as a desperate binge followed by the inevitable hangover is a relatively recent phenomenon beginning, I suspect, around the same time as the first television commercial told us what other people were buying. Prior to that, we set our own agenda, planned ahead and spent what we could afford.

When Christmas gifts were made by hand, preparations began early. It never spoiled the surprise to see your mother knitting mittens, scarves, socks or toques since you didn't know which member of the family they were for. And if your father was spending extra hours in the basement or garage during the fall months, you were smart enough not to go near. Many a sled, doll's house or hobby horse was lovingly hand-crafted whenever time permitted.

Christmas wasn't crammed into a few frantic days. Its magic touched many other parts of the year. Before electricity made its way into our rural areas, bringing strings of coloured lights and plug-in Santas, house and tree decorations were year-round projects. The tinfoil sides of tea packages were saved to wrap cardboard stars, strips of crêpe paper were woven into bells and streamers. The prunings from grape vines were kept for wreath making and the tree itself was often spotted in the woods during the summer, and as you watched it grow and fill out, Christmas was in your thoughts.

Before credit cards turned us into a buy now, pay later society, people actually saved what they could in advance to buy Christmas presents. The Christmas Fund was a popular feature of the workplace; a few dollars were taken from the pay cheque each week and accrued monthly interest until December. This savings-bond type of deduction was a weekly reminder of Christmas joys to come with no guilt or post-holiday debt.

I like to gear down during the month of December. These pre-Christmas days are too precious to spend marching to other people's tunes. It is a month to say no. No to meetings that I can just as well put off until January. No to invitations that I will resent when the date arrives. No to demands that take me away from home. This allows me to say yes. Yes to trying out that new Christmas punch or cookie recipe. Yes for writing newsy letters to neglected friends and relatives. Yes to sharing Christmas stories and singing the beautiful songs of the season with the children in my life.

Some people think Christmas should be over as soon as the turkey bones go into the soup pot. Once the tree is unloaded they can't wait to "get back to normal." Too bad. Christmas has an afterglow that can light our way well into the New Year. The pleasure of giving, renewing friendships and the sheer joy of having fun with the family should not stop when the decorations come down.

Whenever I meet people who think Boxing Day was invented to pack away the previous day, or who can't wait to vacuum up the tinsel, I tell them I'm glad they didn't organize the first Christmas. They would have been very disappointed. The wise men didn't even arrive until January 6.

Has Christmas Gone Too Far?
DECEMBER 1991

Often, I am accused of looking at the past through rose-coloured glasses or of remembering only the good times by painting a brighter picture than actually existed. I deny this. I recall with absolute clarity Christmases that evoked joy and caring without feelings of guilt or frustration.

For one thing, when I was young, money was never a problem in our family because there wasn't any. At least there was none to waste on frivolous purchases. Gifts were home-made and few in number but still received and given with great pleasure. Decorations were designed by the children in the family, hoarded over the years and used to express our festive feelings, not to outdo the efforts of our neighbours. Everyone shared in the preparation of the food and the planning of the entertainment. It was a time of closeness and simple pleasures.

For many years when I was a child, two men came to our door every Christmas morning. Ben and Jim were bachelor brothers who lived on a farm a few concessions west of our place. I would see them occasionally during the year, especially at harvest time or other community activities, dressed in their high-bib overalls and plaid shirts. When they came for their Christmas visit they wore their Sunday-go-to-meeting suits, white shirts and ties.

"Now you folks go right on with your fixin's," they'd say as they made themselves comfortable in our kitchen. "We just thought we'd visit a spell." After a few comments about the weather and everyone's health, my father would go to the cellar for a pitcher of cider and my mother would get out a platter of cookies or cake and Ben and Jim would sit, smiling and watching as we all put the finishing touches on our day's preparations.

Eventually one of them would ask my sister if she still enjoyed playing the piano and this would be a signal for us to adjourn to the parlour where, for the next hour, we would stumble our way through several of the old carols, everyone choosing their favourite. Ben had a deeply rich baritone voice and every year would ask if we would sing "We Three Kings." He so enjoyed coming in between the verses to intone, "And then Caspar spoke" ... "and then

Melchior spoke" … "and then Balthazar spoke." Finally, they would shake all our hands in turn, bashfully give my mother a small box of maple sugar they had boiled down from the sap of their own trees and, calling out a hearty "Merry Chistmas," make their exit.

After Ben and Jim died, I remember asking my mother why they had come to our farm for so many Christmas mornings. I couldn't imagine going somewhere else on this special day. "They never had any family of their own," she explained, "so every year they'd borrow ours for a while." When I pointed out that although they always gave us a gift, we never gave them one, my mother said, "Oh, I believe we did. The best presents are often those you can't wrap."

Have we come too far to go back? I read in my newspaper that the success or failure of our retail economy will depend entirely on Christmas sales this year. In a few weeks when the figures have been tallied we'll know whether our observance of Christ's birth has put us in the black. What's wrong with this picture?

I'm sure I'm not the only one who looks back with fondness to Christmases that were simpler and yet very special. I'll bet your memorable ones have nothing to do with expensive gifts or extravagant celebrations.

Perhaps in the middle of our Christmas preparations we can just pause for a few minutes and ask ourselves, "Is this what I really want to remember about Christmas, and are these the memories I want to pass down to my children?"

A New Twist on Jolly Old Saint Nick

DECEMBER 1993

One of my favourite childhood memories is of the time I first saw Santa Claus. I was seven. I've loved him ever since.

I had heard about him, of course, from my parents' reading of "A Visit from Saint Nicholas," and I saw his picture in magazines and on Christmas cards, but he didn't show up in department stores in those days or ride in parades (at least not in our area). I had no idea what he would be like up close. No doubt he was a very talented person to be able to fly through the air on a sleigh and go down and up all those chimneys in one night.

In a small farming community, you might think people with equally outstanding skills were scarce, but I knew several when I was growing up. There was Mrs. Hogan, for example, who could sing rollicking Irish songs, accompany herself with the spoons and dance a most intricate jig all at the same time. A retired naval officer ran the local feed mill and would hold me spellbound for hours as he told wonderful stories of how brave he had been at the relief of Ladysmith during the Boer War. A farmhand we had could twirl a lasso with astounding precision while jumping back and forth through the loops. I had a cousin who knew the names of all the counties and townships in the province of Ontario and could recite the alphabet backwards. There was really no lack of local talent.

My favourite, though, was Wes Chappel, a young dairy farmer who lived on the Third Concession. He could do handstands, somersaults and cartwheels that left you gasping in amazement. When neighbours got together for the communal haying or threshing bees he would entertain us all by executing mid air flips as he jumped down from the top of the wagons. He had a trapeze hung in his haymow and would willingly perform for us kids as we watched open-mouthed from the opposite loft.

Mr. Chappel was also our Sunday school teacher and many a morning, while he was explaining to us the dos and don'ts of the Ten Commandments, in our mind's eye we were seeing him "fly through the air with the greatest of ease."

The year I was in first grade, it was decided that our one-room rural school was too small for the annual Christmas concert so festivities were moved to the local United Church. The church was only marginally larger, but by pushing the pulpit into the corner and moving the choir pews to one side we were able to make room for parents and siblings who came hoping to see some modicum of talent from the younger generation.

The older grades performed their monologues, skits and humorous recitations. The featured play was the tea party scene from *Alice in Wonderland*, which went very well until the boy playing the dormouse got stuck in a papier-mâché teapot. We smaller kids took part in the singing, marching drills and, dressed up as trees and animals, stood around the crèche while the minister read the Nativity story.

At the end of the evening, a large Christmas tree was lit and everyone was told to sing "Jingle Bells" as loud as possible in preparation for the arrival of Santa Claus. After about the third chorus, each one gaining in volume, I was getting pretty excited. This would be my first view of the jolly old man in person.

Finally the doors of the church flew open and in with the snow and wind came a red-faced, white-haired, ho-ho-hoing Santa. He waved to the cheering, laughing crowd and started toward the tree. Then, wonder of wonders, about halfway down the centre aisle of the church, he leaped into the air, turned an absolutely perfect backflip, landing on his feet as light as a feather.

My eyes bugged. I shouted and clapped my hands. Santa was more wonderful that I could have ever imagined.

I have been a fan of his ever since. After all, he was every bit as good as my talented friend Wes Chappel.

Peace, Goodwill and Matzo-Ball Soup
DECEMBER 1992

Christmas Eve 1950, I wasn't expecting to see Santa Claus. Instead, I heard from someone who gave me a Christmas gift I treasure to this day.

At the time, I was the newest announcer at a small Ontario radio station. Being new and single, I was asked to work the double shift from noon on the twenty-fourth until noon on Christmas Day. This would allow the rest of the staff, mostly married, to spend the time with their families.

It was not a difficult job. Other than the newscasts, most of the programming was pre-selected recordings and taped holiday greetings, so I could manage the 24 hours by myself. Two remote broadcasts, though, made it a long night. We carried a local Christmas Eve church service, then switched to the CBC as they picked up the Midnight Mass from St. Peter's Square in Rome. It was about 2:30 a.m. when I was finally able to read the station sign-off. My plan was to catch some sleep on the couch in the manager's office before signing on again at 6 a.m.

As the final bars of "God Save the King" faded I saw the little red light on the control room phone flash. When I answered, I recognized the gravelly voice of the owner of the Chinese restaurant a few doors from the station. "You must be hungry," he said. "Come over. I'll let you in the back door."

It was cold, dark and windy on the empty streets and I was glad to get inside his warm rich-smelling kitchen where he ladled out a large bowl of steaming soup. "This is matzo-ball soup," he explained. "It's made with crackers and eggs and chicken fat with cinnamon and nutmeg. It's just what we need for a cold night and to help celebrate Hanukkah."

"Are we celebrating Hanukkah?" I asked. In the weeks that I had been coming into his restaurant for hurried lunches or take-out sandwiches and coffee, it had not escaped my curiosity that here was an elderly Jewish immigrant running a Chinese restaurant in small-town Ontario.

"We certainly are. You Christians don't have all the December celebrations. Hanukkah is to remember how we fought to keep our faith. When we light our menorah candles, it recalls the miracle of the oil that lasted eight days when there was only enough for one."

"You must get tired of listening to all that Christmas music I've been playing," I suggested.

"Not at all. I like your Christmas. It talks of peace and goodwill. I come from Germany. I lost my wife and children almost ten years ago. They died in Buchenwald."

I stopped eating. I knew about Buchenwald. I had been announcing news stories about the Nazi death camps, some of which were only now coming to light so long after the war.

The night slipped away as we talked of many things. He told me about his family. He asked me about mine. I explained I would be seeing them for Christmas dinner later that day. He said he would be observing Hanukkah with friends he had made in town.

"It is good to believe," he said. "It is good to have special times to celebrate that belief. If we don't believe the same, what difference does that make? It's like eating. I am a good cook. I can cook any kind of food. Here people like to eat Chinese, so that's what I cook. I appreciate your Christmas and your music. 'Silent Night,' 'Joy to the World.' Even that new one about a reindeer named Rudolph. The world needs happy music."

It was a few minutes to six. I thanked him and ran. As the equipment was warming up, I grabbed the news from the teletype and made a side trip to the library where I pulled out a dusty LP from a special bin. When "O Canada" had finished and a taped devotional prayer came to its "Amen," I slipped the record on the turntable and played the traditional "My Dreidel" (The Spinning Top Song) by a children's chorus.

As I segued into the regular Christmas programs the red light on the phone twinkled. I picked it up and heard his gruff voice say, "Thank you. Happy Hanukkah, my young friend."

"And a Merry Christmas to you, sir," I replied.

Hearing the Message of Christmas Through the Din
DECEMBER 1994

Some people can't stand Christmas music. It often has nothing to do with their religious beliefs, it's just that at this time of year they are being wassailed to death by radio,

TV, department store loudspeakers and elevator mush. Under this constant barrage of discordant jingle and jangle designed primarily as an incentive to buy, buy, buy, they develop an intense dislike for some of the most beautiful music ever written.

At one time, it was my job to program the Christmas season for a Canadian radio station. This involved days of writing, editing and recording Christmas stories and songs for up to 50 pre-recorded shows for use on the twenty-fourth and twenty-fifth of December. Unlike today, where radio simply dumps "Silent Night" into its existing cacophony or where television might use "The Huron Indian Carol" to sell snowmobiles, these programs presented the history of the music and it was performed by favourite artists. There were no commercials even though both days were sold out. A simple sponsor identification at the beginning of each half hour was all that we allowed.

I think knowing a little of the history of a song helps our enjoyment. Take "The First Nowell," for example. It is our most ancient carol. No one actually knows whether it is English or French. It used to be sung in a round like "Row, Row, Row Your Boat," and legend says this type of singing was begun by the angels as one after another joined in the chorus and sung again from the beginning.

There was a Good King Wenceslas, who was much loved by his subjects for his goodness and mercy. Unfortunately his brother Boleslav didn't share that feeling and murdered Wenceslas around 935. John Mason Neale took an old Bohemian "Springtime" tune and transformed it into a Christmas carol honouring the Good King.

One of the best-known carols of Christmas is from an orchestral piece by Felix Mendelssohn that was written in commemoration of the development of the printing press. Anticipating that lyrics would eventually be written for his work, Mendelssohn set down specific instructions. "There must be a national and merry subject found out, something to which the soldier-like and buxom motion of the piece has some relation, and the words must express something gay and popular as the music tries to do." Actually, the words had already been written years before by Charles Wesley. They seemed to be right on target with Mendelssohn's wishes ... "Hark! the Herald Angels Sing, Glory to the Newborn King!"

We are all familiar with "The Twelve Days of Christmas and "A Partridge in a Pear Tree." What many don't know is that the song was originally French, not English, and the gifts were somewhat different. "A stuffing without bones. Two breasts of veal. Three joints of beef. Four pigs. Five legs of mutton. Six partridges with cabbage. Seven spitted rabbits. Eight plates of salad. Nine dishes from the chapter house (whatever that was). Ten full casks. Eleven beautiful maidens ... and twelve musketeers with swords." It's hard to imagine it with no turtledoves or lords a-leaping.

The actual practice of singing carols is believed to have been popularized by a folk tradition of dancing and singing in a circle around a manger scene. The activity was called a crèche. Today we use this word to describe the Nativity scene itself. Even the word *carol* is misused. It comes from the Old French word *carole*, which means round dancing.

Although I've heard people say "If I hear Crosby singing 'White Christmas' once more this year I'll scream," I remember when Irving Berlin said this was his "song of peace, in wartime." He wrote it in 1942 for the movie *Holiday Inn* to remind us that in the terror and hatred of war there is the calmness and love of Christmas. In the years since it has sold more than 200 million copies. No other song even comes close.

It's Not the Cost That Counts
DECEMBER 1996

Some people blame it on the Magi who brought presents to the infant Jesus; historians trace it back further to the Roman Saturnalia. But, whoever started it, gift giving is a wonderful part of this holiday season. It can also be the most frustrating and unhappy part of what is supposed to be a joyous occasion. What bothers me the most is someone giving me a gift that I know they can't afford. I feel embarrassed and uncomfortable, which is exactly opposite to what the person wants me to feel. The phrase "Oh, you

shouldn't have" is heard a lot at Christmas, but sometimes
you really mean it.

The cost of Christmas is going up all the time and most
of us have been guilty of spending more than we really
should on presents. I'm sure I'm not alone when I say I
would like to return to that other hackneyed old expression, "It's the thought that counts." Some families, or co-
workers or groups of friends, draw names for Christmas
giving. A limit is then put on the price of the gift, but as
soon as someone suggests that, say, $10 should be the limit,
someone else will immediately protest, "But you can't buy
anything for $10 these days." Well, they are wrong. It might
take a little thought or some creative shopping, but the
possibilities are endless.

Homemade gifts come immediately to mind, for they
bring with them a message of thoughtfulness that can't be
purchased. A friend of mine drops off a jar of spicy chili
sauce that she made in the fall, a loving reminder of her
kindness long after the holidays are over. A relative makes
up a batch of tangy lemon cheese, which over the years
has become a family tradition. You spoon this into tiny
tart shells and it is the perfect dessert after a heavy festive
dinner. Our Christmas just wouldn't be the same without it.
Dried-flower arrangements, hand-sewn potholders, photographs with special meaning, all prove that it is not just
Hallmark that cares enough to give you their very best.

Those of us who aren't very creative in terms of making

things can still buy presents that won't put us in hock come the New Year. That book that was on the bestseller list last Christmas is now out in paperback this year and reads exactly the same. And some real literary treasures are found in second-hand bookstores, where favourite authors can be rediscovered and shared. At this time of year, many organizations, community groups and schools hold bazaars or craft sales to raise money for charitable causes. Choosing a gift here gives extra value to the few dollars you spend. The person receiving your present will not only appreciate your thoughtfulness but knowing where you bought it will add warmth and joy that have no price tag.

Gifts for children present special problems. They have seen so many advertisements for the latest costly toy fad that anything else under the tree can be a disappointment. Usually, though, a straightforward explanation of spending limits can convince a child that there are plenty of other delightful gifts available. But it takes time and thought. One of the worst Christmases ever for me happened when I was ten and I unwrapped a bottle of hair tonic and a packet of war-savings stamps.

Even with the best of intentions you can still cause grief. When my daughter Mandy was 12, I gave her a Christmas gift that I thought was ideal. It was a music box with a carving of a young girl wistfully staring into space as she twirled around to the strains of "Lara's Theme" from the movie *Doctor Zhivago*. Even though she tried her best to hide it, the disappointment on her face when she opened the gift broke my heart. She was obviously expecting something else.

But it really is the thought that counts. I realized later that the gift of hair tonic was to make me feel grown-up and special. The war-savings stamps were to help me feel part of the school crowd who could afford to buy them when I couldn't. Mandy now says her music box is the one gift that has remained into adulthood and has a place of honour in her home.

It's obviously not the cost, but the caring.

ONE FINAL NOTE ...

I have asked that royalties from the sale of this book be donated to F.A.C.E. (Families and Children Experiencing) AIDS.

An estimated 900 Canadian women have AIDS or have died from it. Canadian women with AIDS have contracted the HIV virus in these ways:

- Heterosexual contact, 64 per cent
- Blood and blood products, 16 per cent
- Injection drug use, 11 per cent
- Unknown, 9 per cent

Up to 10 per cent of the 28,000 to 35,000 Canadians who are estimated to be infected with HIV are women, and most of them do not know they have it. Between 12 per cent and 28 per cent of infected women are going to transmit the virus to their newborn children. About 80 per cent of all children known to be infected acquired the virus by transmission from their mothers.

F.A.C.E. AIDS is an incorporated, non-profit charity dedicated to helping these children and their families in any way it can. I am proud to be its national spokesperson.